# TALENT
# GENERATION

How *visionary organizations*
are *redefining work*
and *achieving greater success*

## SARAH L. SLADEK

association
management
press

WASHINGTON, DC

The author has worked diligently to ensure that all information in this book is accurate as of the time of publication and consistent with standards of good practice in the general management community. As research and practice advance, however, standards may change. For this reason it is recommended that readers evaluate the applicability of any recommendations in light of particular situations and changing standards.

ASAE: The Center for Association Leadership
1575 I Street, NW
Washington, DC 20005-1103
Phone: (202) 626-2723; (888) 950-2723 outside metropolitan Washington, DC area
Fax: (202) 220-6439
Email: books@asaecenter.org

We connect great ideas and great people to inspire leadership and achievement in the association community.

Keith C. Skillman, CAE, Vice President, Publications, ASAE: The Center for Association Leadership
Baron Williams, CAE, Director of Book Publishing, ASAE: The Center for Association Leadership

Cover and text design by Troy Scott Parker, Cimarron Design

This book is available at a special discount when ordered in bulk quantities. For information, contact the ASAE Member Service Center at (202) 371-0940. A complete catalog of titles is available on the ASAE website at www.asaecenter.org.

# Contents

# *Dedication*

This book is dedicated to:

My father, who often brought me to work with him. When I was 13, he asked me to make a list of suggestions for how he, a bank president, could improve his workplace. I was surprised when, a year later, he showed me where he kept the list in his desk, and that he completed each of my suggestions. Thank you, Dad, for teaching me the value of listening to others, the importance of being humble and honest, and showing me how to lead with conviction and care.

My husband, who owned his first business by the age of 23. A few companies later, he decided to sell his own businesses to join mine. Thank you, Brad, for being fearless. I have learned so much from you and greatly admire your determination, dedication, vision, and faith. Thank you for believing in me—and for coming up with the title of this book!

My daughters, who inspire me and teach me something new every day, reminding me that when it comes to readying the world for the next generation, society's work is never done.

All the rebels and the visionaries. Thank you for refusing to settle or stick to the status quo. Thank you for mentoring and inspiring future generations. Thank you for seeking to leave a legacy that really matters, passing your organization on, and creating some of meaning, value, and importance to the next generation.

And to the young people. Be brave. Never underestimate your ability. Never lose sight of your extraordinary gifts. Your generation is unique, and that's powerful. A better future is yours to inspire and create.

# A Call to Action

I feel a little bit like Chicken Little telling you we're in a workforce crisis. You've read the research and headlines, but if you're like most people, you don't want to believe it.

After all, employee engagement and profitability have been declining since 1965, and people still get up and go to work and companies still make billions of dollars every day. Nothing has changed and it never will. Right?

Ironically, on the day I'm writing this introduction, it's Earth Day 2017 and scientists and protesters are rallying around the world in a rebuke of President Donald Trump's dismissal of climate science and attempts to cut large areas of scientific research.

Some people don't believe in climate change, and some don't believe we're in a workforce crisis either. But for those of you who *are* concerned about finding and keeping talent and want to create a better future for your organizations, this book is for you. I wrote this book to serve as a guide to the organizations seeking to navigate their way out of this workforce crisis toward greater success.

And for those of you who are still not convinced a workforce crisis exists, allow me the opportunity to try a different tactic to convince you:

Picture your local hospital. Think about the people who work there and the work they do. What would happen if that hospital closed? What if the health clinics closed and there were no medical professionals left in your community either? Can you imagine your community without access to any healthcare whatsoever? How would that change your life?

The fact is, healthcare is now the fastest-growing industry in the nation, partly because people are living longer and partly because the Baby Boomer generation—the largest generation of the 20th century and the largest percentage of the healthcare workforce—is now entering their retirement years.

So, more healthcare is needed than ever before, at a time when hospitals and clinics are struggling to find and keep talent more than ever before.

In 2016, *The Atlantic* reported that an estimated 700,000 nurses will retire or leave the workforce within the next seven years. Already, hospitals in the United States lose an average of $5-8 million annually in employee turnover costs, and this turnover is most rampant among young people. As a result, employee retention has become the strategic imperative for 90 percent of U.S. hospitals.

The bottom line: There aren't enough young workers to replace the retiring workers. Wait—let me rephrase that. There *are* enough young workers, but they don't want to work in the same jobs, doing the same type of work, answering to the same types of leaders, in the same organizational cultures as their predecessors. And when an organization can't engage the talent it needs, the results can be dire.

A University of South Carolina healthcare report candidly stated, "there will be deaths and unintentional injuries" as a direct result of the state's nursing shortage. The state of South Carolina is already experiencing a shortage of 2,000 nurses, with a projected loss of 6,800 nurses within the next 10 years.

Healthcare isn't the only industry challenged with a workforce crisis. It's apparent in every industry and it's a global concern.

The crisis isn't due to a lack of smart, ambitious, innovative people. It's a crisis that we, as leaders, could solve ourselves, because the crisis stems from organizations and their cultures. Quite simply, the workforce crisis is the result of an ever-widening gap between the Industrial Era 20th century-managed organizations, and the Post-Industrial 21st century-raised workforce.

In the 20th century, the economy was fueled by natural resources and structured by hierarchy. Now, we're well into the 21st century, a talent-driven economy characterized by knowledge, innovation, globalization, mobility, and customization, but too few organizations have shifted away from 20th century workforce practices. With a 21st century generation now composing the majority of the workforce, employee turnover has accelerated and the workforce crisis has worsened.

This book will demonstrate that many organizations simply lack the structure, strategy, and culture to manage employees effectively in the 21st century. To succeed, several factors need to be modernized and addressed, including the relevance of people and profits; changing demographics and evolving definitions of work; leadership ability and cultivation; future planning; and talent development.

As we move from the computer age into the cyber age, the workforce crisis will become even more apparent as new industries, jobs, and skills emerge. The real issue is no longer talent management; it's talent generation. It's imperative that organizations engage younger generations of talent, and help train and prepare future talent.

There is, perhaps, no other organization better suited to solve the workforce crisis than membership associations. Associations represent thousands of businesses and millions of employees. Associations represent industry interests in government and education. Finally, associations have the power and influence to create real and meaningful change. Businesses will be looking to associations to help solve the workforce crisis.

This isn't just another cautionary tale. It's a call to action. This isn't someone else's problem to solve. It's yours and mine. Every membership association, business, government, nonprofit, and country needs to own this problem and make it a priority to resolve it.

Without talent, we have much to lose. Without talent, we have no purpose, no future, and no hope. Without talent, society fails. So let's put an end to the workforce crisis. Let's make work work again.

Welcome, dear reader, to talent generation. I guarantee this will be the most important job you've ever had.

*"Lots of companies don't succeed over time.*
*What do they fundamentally do wrong?*
*They usually miss the future."*

LARRY PAGE

CHAPTER 1

......................

# Mind the Gaps

The following is an excerpt from a speech I presented at a corporate event in 2015:

> Early in my career, I was hired to be the managing editor of a daily business newspaper. I remember my first day on that job well.
>
> Being the managing editor meant that I was ultimately responsible for everything affiliated with the newsroom, from determining what stories to cover, to managing the staff, design, production, budget, and operations.
>
> On that first day as I walked around and introduced myself to everyone I quickly realized I was one of the youngest people on the staff, not just in the newsroom, but in the entire building. Upon introducing myself as the new managing editor, some people laughed, some ignored me. One person chastised me, saying "You're the new editor? Give me a break. I've been working at this place longer than you've been alive."

At the end of the day I walked into the publisher's office, shut the door behind me and tried to contain my panic. I rambled something like this: "Today was a bit difficult. You may not have realized this when you hired me, but I'm only 25 years old, and I'm guessing after today that I'm one of two or three people in this entire building under the age of 35! Did you know that you'd be asking me to manage people twice my age? People who really don't want me managing them? I mean, I've managed people before, but there wasn't such an age gap. I just didn't expect this to be the situation and I'm a bit worried."

The publisher took this in, pondered it, then leaned forward and said: "I'm worried too. In fact, I haven't been able to sleep the past few nights I've been so worried. I mean let's be honest. You are green."

Somehow this really wasn't making me feel any better. The publisher went on.

"Look, I didn't want to like you. I interviewed a lot of people for this job, but the fact is you were the best qualified. So I decided to take a risk and I hired you. You can do this job. It's not going to be easy, but you can do it. I'm counting on you—so get back out there and prove me right."

So I did. And the publisher was right. That job wasn't easy; hands down it was the most difficult job I've ever had. But that's not the point. Ladies and gentlemen, as I stand before you today, I'd like to invite you to contemplate that leader's decision—the decision to take a risk and hire someone young.

It's worth pondering because the fact is, far too few leaders are opting to do this at a time when our nation desperately needs to escape the norm and nurture young talent.

Presently every single sector, with the exception of technology, is predominantly managed by Baby Boomers (born 1946–1964). This is really no surprise. When they came of age, the Boomers were the largest generation in history and had the opportunity to move into positions of power and influence and stay there.

However, for the first time in several decades, Boomers are no longer the majority. It is now Generation Y, also known as Millennials. To put that in perspective, this year Gen Ys will turn between the ages of 20 and 33. That means the majority of our workforce is now in their 20s.

We're on the brink of the largest shift in human capital in history, yet one generation still holds nearly all the power in nearly every sector in nearly every corner of the world and the proverbial baton isn't getting passed.

Executive research projects continually draw the same conclusion: succession planning isn't a priority for 70 percent of executives.

Ladies and gentlemen, it's time to really think about leadership, both who is leading and how we're leading, because our leaders are aging and our current leadership practices are failing.

To be honest, I was nervous about presenting this speech. I present often, but this was different. The CEO and members of the executive team had seated themselves in the center of the front row of the auditorium, and I wasn't sure how they would respond to my presentation. It's not easy to stand on stage, a mere few feet away from someone, look them in the eye, and tell them they are on the wrong path.

But that's exactly what I did, and it's exactly what I know to be true: Our leadership is aging, our leadership practices are failing, and it's time for people to start speaking up about it and resolving it.

Little did I know that when that publisher took a chance on me, it would light a fire in my very soul, bringing a sudden and somewhat painful realization that being young and being given the opportunity to lead isn't common practice. At least it wasn't in 1996.

Shortly thereafter, at the age of 27, I moved into another leadership role. I attended a national directors' conference and was mistaken for someone's daughter.

Again, I couldn't shake the feeling that organizations were making a grave mistake by refusing to give young people a voice, much less leadership opportunities, amidst an era of great disruption and technological advancements. It seemed to me that increasing the diversity of skillsets was key to navigating and succeeding in the 21st century; something to be celebrated, not feared. But I struggled to find organizations that shared this same perspective, and even fewer were putting it into practice.

This book is based on 16 years of workforce research. No longer just a hunch, I've identified one very significant truth: Any organization that wants to succeed in the 21st century must provide a means for entry-level talent to work in close collaboration with executive-level talent.

## The Emergence of Talent

The year was 2000. The startup that launched in 1998 had outgrown the garage, and was relocating to a nondescript building in an office park a couple of miles off the highway.

Outside that building, on an asphalt parking lot, yellow police tape marked off an area where employees played roller hockey. The games were full contact. Employees wore pads and would come back inside drenched in sweat and sometimes bloodied and bruised. The harder you played, the more respect you earned.

Inside the building, the game was twice as tough. Yes, there was free food for all employees and a massage therapist on site. And with brightly colored exercise balls and couches everywhere, the place looked like a kindergarten class crossed with a freshman dorm. The tough part was the company's founder, who would often provoke arguments with the staff over business and product decisions.

It wasn't that he was a tyrant. It just became very apparent that he connected to people over their ideas and not their feelings. After all, Larry Page once told a co-worker his method for solving complex problems was by reducing them to binaries, then simply choosing the best option. He managed in the same no-nonsense way, pushing his employees to develop their visions of future technologies. For most, this combative atmosphere was a reasonable price to pay for working at a company with a real clarity of purpose.

A few years after the idea of ranking web pages by their inbound links came to Page in a dream, the founder of Google wrote down his five rules for management. He was in his twenties at the time.

1. Don't delegate. Do everything you can yourself to make things go faster.

2. Don't get in the way if you're not adding value. Let the people actually doing the work talk to each other while you go do something else.

3. Don't be a bureaucrat.

4. Ideas are more important than age. Just because someone is junior doesn't mean they don't deserve respect and cooperation.

5. The worst thing you can do is stop someone from doing something by saying, "No." If you say no, you have to help them find a better way to get it done.

This unrelenting focus on ideas, outcomes, employee empowerment, and purpose had never existed before, and Google is still known today for having a workplace culture that is truly revolutionary.

Somewhere at the tail end of the 20th century—perhaps right in that asphalt parking lot where the first Google employees played roller hockey—the economy pivoted and two radical changes occurred. Suddenly, it became apparent that young people have valuable skills and talent to offer; and you could write your own rules for management. And these two realizations led to an inevitable outcome: Talent would soon become our nation's most precious and elusive resource.

Let's pause for a moment to contemplate the significance of this shift. Prior to this shift, work was just a job, leadership was the equivalent of power, and the prioritization of talent didn't really exist. Consider this timeline:

### 1910

Natural resources were a company's most valuable assets: Standard Oil needed hydrocarbons, U.S. Steel needed iron ore and coal, the Great Atlantic & Pacific Tea Company needed real estate. America's leading companies grew large by spending increasing amounts of capital to acquire and exploit oil, mineral deposits, forests, water, and land.

### 1946

In the post-World War II-era, companies took a lesson from the military and applied systems to absolutely everything for increased efficiency, predictability, and productivity. This management move piggy-backed on the Industrial Era management practices already in play, resulting in a command-and-control leadership style that Baby Boomers (1946–1964) were raised knowing. This style of leadership is systems and process-oriented and rooted in hierarchy. Senior management has both privilege and power, and the intent is to maintain predictability and drive profits at the risk of adaptability, inclusion, and innovation.

**1955**

An insatiable appetite for American-made cars spurred both the natural resources and manufacturing industries. Listed among the ten largest employers that year were GM, Chrysler, U.S. Steel, Standard Oil of New Jersey, Amoco, Goodyear, and Firestone. These types of companies needed lots of labor as they continued to grow—but mainly for routine-intensive jobs. When turnover occurred, those jobs were easy to fill and individual workers had little bargaining power. Labor took a distant third place in the economic pecking order, behind natural resources and providers of capital.

**1963**

A relatively new breed of corporation arrived to the list of 20 largest companies in the United States: IBM. Although the company began operations as a computing/tabulating/recording company in 1911, it hit its stride in the '60s, making and selling massive computers to large governments and corporations. IBM was unique in that it was a technology company, but also in that it wasn't reliant on automation or natural resources. Rather, scientists, engineers, marketers, and salespeople were at the heart of IBM's competitive advantage.

**1965**

Business growth dominated the economy, and more jobs began to require creativity, as well as independent judgment and decision-making skills. The concept of talent (utilizing skills, knowledge, and ideas) began to emerge, and Generation X (1965–1981) was born. Generation Y (1982–1995), also known as Millennials, would follow, renowned for being

both the first generation raised in a technology-driven era
and the largest generation in history.

### 1998

Google was founded by Larry Page and Sergey Brin, ages
25 and 24 respectively, ushering in an era of rule-breaking
and innovation among people who would have once been
regarded as too young to lead or influence.

### 2016

Topping the 50 largest companies list were Apple, Microsoft,
and Google, all talent-focused companies. Only two
companies owed their position on the list to the ownership
of natural resources. For the fourth time in a row, *Fortune*'s
list of the World's Most Admired Companies was led by a
trio of tech giants all under 40 years old: Apple, Alphabet,
and Amazon. Start-up empires had become the norm. In
fact, according to the 2016 BNP Paribas Global Entrepreneur
Report, people under the age of 35 were starting more
companies, managing bigger staffs, and realizing higher
profits than any of their predecessors. Some of the start-up
wave is linked to new technologies, but it's also representative of a bigger shift that has taken place, which now
accepts that you can be the CEO of a big company or own
your own company at a young age.

This brings me back to my previous point. The economy's
decreasing reliance on automation and natural resources and the
emergence of technology gave rise to the Talent Economy, an era
driven by a collaborative, innovative, mobile, on-demand workforce
fueled by ideas and information. Suddenly it became apparent
that young people have valuable talent to offer and the rules of
management could be rewritten.

In other words, the Talent Economy has given influence to young people who possess great ambition or ideas, and leaders willing to take risks, drive change, and ditch the status quo. By themselves, each of these are powerful forces, but when they work together, it leads to even greater success.

Young professionals and experienced leaders working together sounds easy enough, perhaps even obvious. But this practice has proven to be quite difficult, and in many cases vastly overlooked.

## A Generation Gap

Three generations dominate the current workforce: Baby Boomers (1946–1964), Generation X (1965–1981), and Generation Y, also known as Millennials (1982–1995). As this book is being written, Generation Z (1996–2009) is just beginning to enter the workforce.

At the end of 2015, Millennials (ages 22–35 in 2017) became the workforce majority. This transition marked the largest shift in human capital in history; for the first time in 34 years the Baby Boomers were no longer the workforce majority.

This massive shift in human capital caused big problems for even the most successful companies. Employee turnover has become a major concern, costing U.S. companies an estimated $30.5 billion per year, according to Gallup. As a result, Millennials have been type-casted as the most difficult workforce in history, and they also happen to be the most studied generation in history. But rather than dismissing this generation as unmotivated, lazy, disloyal, and entitled, it's crucial to look at the larger macro trends in play.

Millennials, and the generations that follow, have little to no memory of Industrial Era or command-and-control methodologies and therefore no appreciation or understanding of processes, hierarchy, and doing things the way they've always been done.

This is a generation that was born into and has only known a world powered by the trademarks of a Talent Economy: innovation,

interconnectedness, globalization, and opportunity. Anything else
will seem foreign and irrelevant to them. They will struggle to
comprehend why the bylaws can't be changed, why decisions can't
be made on the fly, why they can't have a seat at the decision-making
table, and why it's always been done "that way."

| Industrial Era | Talent Economy |
|---|---|
| *Boomers and Xers* | *Millennials and Gen Z* |
| Hierarchy | Collaboration |
| Profits | People |
| Experience | Innovation |
| Reliable | Adaptable |
| Manage | Lead |
| Maintain | Disrupt |
| Work | Purpose |
| Past | Future |

Consider that Millennials are the first generation of the
Post-Industrial Era, raised in a world driven by technology and
globalization. They came of age during the Great Recession—the worst
economic decline our country had experienced in 70 years—and they
are the best-educated generation in history, and the most protected
and supervised generation in history. They have delayed marriage and
parenthood longer than other generations, partly for financial reasons
and partly to pursue advanced degrees.

These characteristics have shaped this generation's career
trajectory, making Millennials more likely to change jobs than
previous generations. XYZ University's research of U.S. Millennials
reveals they have spent more time than other generations exploring
careers and opportunities for advancement for two key reasons:

1. They are searching for jobs that tap into their Post-Industrial values for education and collaboration; and

2. They are still reeling from the recession, paying off student loans, and seeking jobs that will allow them to support themselves financially.

The Deloitte Millennial Survey, which surveyed nearly 7,700 Millennials in 29 countries, revealed that 44 percent of this generation plans to leave their jobs within the next two years, 25 percent within one year. To date, Millennials have changed jobs three times more frequently than older generations of workers.

Several factors play into this loyalty challenge, according to Deloitte:

• Young professionals feel most businesses have no ambition beyond profit; and

• The majority (63 percent) of young professionals said their leadership skills are not being fully developed by their current employer.

Clearly, the values of this generation aren't aligning with most employee experiences.

If organizations want to recruit and retain young professionals and compete in the Talent Economy, organizations will need to adapt.

But let's face it. Few companies are powered by innovation in the same way as Google. Hence, we have a problem: an ever-widening gap between the Industrial Era 20th century-managed companies, and the Post Industrial 21st century-raised workforce.

Consider these Millennial stats, as a result of being raised in the Talent Economy:

• 92 percent believe business success should be measured by more than profit (Deloitte);

- 81 percent have donated money, goods, or services (Walden University and Harris Interactive);

- 80 percent prefer on-the-spot recognition over formal reviews (Achievers and Experience Inc);

- 72 percent want a job where they can make an impact (Millennial Branding);

- 71 percent seek meaningful relationships at work (Gallup);

- 70 percent have "friended" their managers and/or co-workers on Facebook (Cisco);

- 56 percent wouldn't work for a company that bans social media (Cisco);

- On average, they carry $45,000 in debt (Business Insider);

- When asked to describe the ideal leader, most use the words honest, innovative, inspiring (XYZ University).

This generation is now the majority of the workforce, outnumbering even the Baby Boomer generation, and will represent 75 percent of the global workforce by 2025. Knowing what this emerging market needs and values most is critical to your organization's success.

## The Employee Engagement Gap

Despite all the data on employee turnover, the Millennials aren't solely to blame for our workforce woes. The fact is, long before the Millennials arrived on the scene and the largest shift in human capital took place, much ink was being spilled on the challenges of disruption and employee engagement.

Gallup has been tracking employee engagement since 2000. Though there have been slight ebbs and flows, less than one third of U.S. employees have been engaged in their jobs and workplaces during the past 17 years. According to Gallup, 32 percent of employees in the

## Mind the Gaps Quiz

Does your organization have what it takes to engage the next generation?
Take this quick quiz to find out.

| | |
|---|---|
| Our workforce/members/ volunteers know our organization's purpose and why their participation matters.<br>□ True<br>□ False | Most people would describe our organization as happy, welcoming, and fun.<br>□ True<br>□ False |
| Younger people are frequently invited to share their opinions and ideas with the leadership team.<br>□ True<br>□ False | Our leadership team actively uses social media.<br>□ True<br>□ False |
| We think and act fast as an organization.<br>□ True<br>□ False | Most people would describe our leaders as innovative and inspiring.<br>□ True<br>□ False |
| We allow employees time off for volunteering.<br>□ True<br>□ False | Most people would describe our leaders as honest and trustworthy.<br>□ True<br>□ False |
| We offer tuition reimbursement and scholarships to young people.<br>□ True<br>□ False | We spend more time thinking about the future than the present or the past.<br>□ True<br>□ False |

If you answered false to any of the questions above, that likely represents a gap hindering your organization's ability to engage young talent.

United States are engaged, meaning they are involved in, enthusiastic about, and committed to their work and workplace. Worldwide, only 13 percent of employees are engaged.

That's not all, there's more.

Every year since 1987, the Conference Board has conducted a job satisfaction survey. In 1987, some 61 percent of workers said they liked their jobs. Since then, job satisfaction has been on a steady decline. Today, only 49 percent of employees are happy at work.

In addition, Deloitte's Shift Index studied the performance of 20,000 U.S. organizations between 1965 and 2016. It shows a general picture of performance decline over the 51 years. In fact, despite a soaring stock market, in 2016 the rate of return on assets (ROA) of these firms was only one quarter of what it was in 1965. In other words, profitability declined by 75 percent. To combat a negative ROA trend in the short-term, companies often resort to cost cutting, layoffs, or outsourcing. But these measures haven't been effective at reversing the profitability trend.

Moreover, the Shift Index reports that worker passion is incredibly low. Deloitte defines worker passion as a continuing commitment to accomplishment, a disposition to quest and explore, and an openness to connect with others. Presently, a mere 13 percent of workers are passionate about their work.

The bottom line: Employee engagement and profitability have been declining since 1965. If that's not enough to make your stomach churn, then I'm not sure what will. These are serious shortcomings.

Why is this happening? Because our leadership is aging, our management practices are failing, and the gap between executive-level and entry-level talent has continued to widen. For starters, we inherited institutions designed for the 20th century, which are unable to cope with the mounting pressures of constant change. Many organizations are still structured to maximize efficiency by way of clearly defined roles, which automatically creates resistance to any variance.

Whether they realize it or not, many companies today are structured such that they actively discourage passion. Think about it. In the 20th century, corporations were built for scalable efficiency. Jobs were well-defined and organized to support processes designed to meet plans and forecasts. Workers were trained to protect company information. Any collaboration with those outside of the organization was highly monitored or even discouraged. Most innovation was driven from within the company's four walls, often without feedback or customer interaction.

Now we've moved into the 21st century—the Talent Economy. And today's creative, passionate workers certainly don't want to work in Industrial-Era organizations with clearly defined roles, organizational silos, top-down management, or predictability.

Signals you're working for a 20th century institution may include any of the following:

- Morale appears low.
- People are leaving the organization.
- When asked "Why do you work here?", employees refer to the insurance plan.
- The CFO spends 5 percent of the time talking about revenue growth and 95 percent talking about cutting costs.
- New opportunities are evaluated and dismissed based on their impact to the old legacy business.
- Your managers are unengaged in conversations about how new technologies like Apple Watches, Twitter, and Amazon Web Services will affect your organization.

- You spend the first week of the quarter talking about long-term strategic planning, then the next 12 weeks scrambling to make the quarter.

- All conversations about new growth end with reluctant middle management saying, "Only if you give me more budget!"

- The budget never comes, and you all go back to what you were doing.

In the turbulent competitive marketplace of the 21st century, organizations need workers with passion to realize extreme sustained performance improvement. We need leaders who are willing to disrupt the status quo, working in collaboration with young professionals willing to innovate and bring new solutions to the forefront.

We need talent generation.

## Talent Generation

This book will highlight several examples of organizations that have thrown out tradition to recruit, retain, and raise talent, realizing talent and innovation are now every company's greatest asset.

Unfortunately, these examples are too few and far between. The inability for most organizations to evolve has led to failure of epic proportions. While holding steadfast to former practices, businesses observed increases in employee turnover, membership associations observed membership decline, the workforce grew miserable, the economy sputtered and crashed, and political issues continued to be unfixable.

Our leadership is aging. We cannot continue along this path of total dominance on one end of the age spectrum. If we fail to engage future generations, who are now the majority of our workforce, we prepare to fail. After all, they are our only succession plan.

Our talent practices are failing. We cannot continue to hold onto the past. Many organizations are struggling today simply because the leadership tries to apply 20th century management practices to a 21st century workforce. For too long, we've just assumed there is no better way and it is impossible to engage today's young talent.

But clearly, there is another way. All I have to do is mention the word "Google" and you know what I'm talking about. I mentioned Larry Page's rules for management earlier. Employees are drawn to Google because working there means something more than "just" working for an internet service and product company. In fact, Google is successful for reasons that have very little to do with what the company actually does.

Google was built on the premise that people want meaningful work, knowledge of what's happening in their environment, and the opportunity to shape that environment. Simply put, Google put its employees at the center of everything. And success has certainly followed. Google has grown into a business earning $50 billion in revenues and continually earns honors as the best company to work for in the United States, Canada, Japan, India, Korea, and Brazil. Google embodies the two trademarks of a 21st century organization: People First and Future-Focused.

Companies that put people first value people more than anything—even profits. Companies that are future-focused are visionary and innovative and give younger generations an empowering, influential role in the development of the organization.

When more leaders make a conscious decision and take appropriate action to value people more than profits, and invest in the next generation of talent; that's when we will not only succeed at collaboration and innovation, it's when we will reverse the decline, resolve the conflicts, and ultimately prevent our economy from failing.

That publisher who decided to take a risk and hire me? I later found out the publisher had to convince the newspaper's owner and board of directors to hire me. I later found out I was the youngest person

and the only female on record to have held that leadership role.
So indeed, I was a risk. And yet, the publisher advocated for me to
have the opportunity to lead. Now I ask you, isn't that every leader's
responsibility?

Leaders, the best ones, set an example of fairness and credibility,
have the vision and willingness to break out of the norm, and remain
open-minded to new ideas and solutions. The best leaders add value
to an organization, not slow it down or kill initiative. The best leaders
realize they don't have all the answers, and will benefit from the
insights of a younger generation, raised amidst disruption and rapidly
evolving technology and seeing the world through a different lens.
Which is why we desperately need leaders who are willing to disrupt
the status quo and work alongside and advocate on behalf of younger
generations.

Whether you realize it or not, leadership is the biggest single
determinant of your quality of life. With the $30 billion turnover
epidemic spurred by the Millennial generation, they have proven
they won't settle for anything less than visionary, collaborative, and
inspiring leadership.

And don't overlook the fact that we've been on this path since 1965.
Employee engagement and productivity have steadily been declining
for more than 50 years, and few have raised their voices in opposition
or dedicated themselves to initiating a change.

Ladies and gentlemen, it's time to think about leadership, because
our leadership is aging and our talent practices are failing. It's time for
a change. It's time to make the future a priority, for every generation.

**CHAPTER SUMMARY**

The economy's decreasing reliance on automation and natural resources and the emergence of technology gave rise to the Talent Economy, an era driven by a collaborative, innovative, mobile, on-demand workforce fueled by ideas and information.

The Talent Economy has given influence to young people who possess great ambition or ideas, and leaders willing to take risks, drive change, and ditch the status quo. By themselves, each of these are powerful forces, but when they work together, it leads to even greater success.

**QUESTIONS TO CONSIDER**

1. Refer to the chart on page 10. Is your organization rooted in Industrial Era practices or Talent Economy practices? If you answered Industrial Era, what's holding the organization back from becoming a Talent Economy organization?

2. What are some of the generational differences you've observed in your organization?

3. If those generational differences were resolved, how would that change your organization?

4. Review Larry Page's list of management rules listed below. On a scale of 1–5 (1 being awful and 5 being awesome) how would you rank your organization's current proficiency at following each of these rules?

   _____ Don't delegate. Do everything you can yourself to make things go faster.

   _____ Don't get in the way if you're not adding value. Let the people actually doing the work talk to each other while you go do something else.

   _____ Don't be a bureaucrat.

\_\_\_\_ Ideas are more important than age. Just because someone is junior doesn't mean they don't deserve respect and cooperation.

\_\_\_\_ The worst thing you can do is stop someone from doing something by saying, "No." If you say no, you have to help them find a better way to get it done.

5. What one thing could your organization do (or stop doing) that would make a tremendous difference to the employee experience?

6. If your organization is a membership association, what services could the association provide to help member companies bridge generational gaps and engage more young professionals?

*The Talent Generation model provides a visual illustration of the key components of the steps outlined in this book, and the steps an organization must take to achieve employee engagement, growth, and relevance in the Talent Economy. This model applies to every size and type of organization.*

Build the Future
Education and Business Align

Leadership
Passion, Optimism, Humility, Urgency

Collaborate
Innovation via Team-Building

Acceptance
Inclusion and Trust

Future Focus
Research, Trends, Opportunities

People First
Mission, Vision, and Strategy

> *"A leader's job is to look into the future and see the organization, not as it is, but as it should be."*
>
> JACK WELCH

..............................

## CHAPTER 2

# Start at the Top

Mark Zuckerberg was a superstar student at Harvard, a computer prodigy who was able, in his spare time, to bang out the lines of code that would become Facebook, a transformational social networking company.

In 2012, eight years after Facebook was founded, Zuckerberg faced his first big test as a CEO—Facebook's initial public offering of stock. It didn't go well. Shares were priced too high and too many of them were on the market, so instead of getting the typical IPO "pop," Facebook's stock swooned. Then came a bombshell that the company, worried about a weakening business, had quietly warned Wall Street analysts to lower their projections in the days before the IPO. Privileged clients got the news and backed away from the stock, while everyone else remained in the dark and rushed in to buy the shares. Some early-in-the-day investors lost 25 percent overnight.

In the end, Zuckerberg was widely criticized for being too immature to run a massive corporation.

An article in *Newsweek* reported "the baby-faced 28-year-old flunked, and badly," referring to it as an overhyped and poorly managed stock deal, noting the "wunderkind hacker appeared to be in way over his head." A Stanford Law School research fellow was quoted: "Facebook has gone from being a darling to being a villain. Zuckerberg went from being seen as this child-genius rock star to being seen as a thief." A research firm analyst referred to Zuckerberg's lack of education as cause for concern. (Zuckerberg dropped out of Harvard shortly after launching Facebook during his sophomore year.)

Perhaps the most controversial and disconcerting part of the IPO roadshow was not what Zuckerberg did, but what he wore. Zuckerberg is known for his ever-present hoodie, t-shirt, and sandals. In Facebook's early days, he once showed up for a meeting with a venture-capital firm in his pajamas. The young CEO broke hoodie/pajama tradition in 2009, when he wore a tie every day. On his Facebook timeline Zuckerberg wrote: "After the start of the recession in 2008, I wanted to signal to everyone at Facebook that this was a serious year for us. My tie was the symbol of how serious and important a year this was, and I wore it every day to show this."

Perhaps Zuckerberg, sitting on the verge of a blockbuster stock offering, no longer felt the need to prove himself. But it was obvious no one on Wall Street expected him to show up for the IPO wearing a hoodie. An analyst told Bloomberg TV Zuckerberg's decision to dress in casual outerwear for the IPO suggested that "he doesn't care that much" which is a "mark of immaturity." He went on to say that Zuckerberg might be a better product manager or designer than CEO. Facebook's stock lost nearly half its value in the weeks following the IPO. Zuckerberg saw the value of his Facebook holding fall by more than $9 billion.

Two years later, Zuckerberg held his first-ever public Q&A session. He answered a lot of questions, but the one that got a lot of interest was, "Why do you wear the same t-shirt every day?" While many expected a playful response, Zuckerberg gave a pretty serious answer:

> I really want to clear my life, to make it so that I have to make as few decisions as possible about anything except

how to best serve this community. ... I'm in this really lucky position where I get to wake up every day and help serve more than a billion people. And I feel like I'm not doing my job if I spend any of my energy on things that are silly or frivolous about my life.

I'm sharing this story with you because it's the perfect example of the collision we're observing in today's workforce. Mark Zuckerberg wasn't considered CEO material. He wasn't the right age. He didn't take the right path or have the right education. He didn't take his time or follow traditions, and he certainly didn't wear the right clothes.

Zuckerberg is representative of the Talent Economy, the Post-Industrial Era characterized by innovation, disruption, and considerably less regard to formalities and traditions. Zuckerberg is committed to doing it his way. Experience isn't his advantage; ideas and innovation are.

However, many organizations today are structured in such a way that they still consider experience the sole advantage. That's because in the 20th century, organizations were built for efficiency; most innovation was driven from within the company's four walls, and leadership was reserved for those with the most experience.

Not surprising, in this 21st century Talent Economy, a chasm occurs when experience is perceived to be the sole competitive advantage, sometimes even to the point of avoiding new ideas, strategies, and approaches. It shouldn't be a competition: experience vs. innovation. It needs to be a collaboration. We shouldn't be making it harder for young people to succeed, standing at the ready to criticize them for their mistakes or inexperience.

The gap between executive-level (experienced, 20th century) and entry-level (innovative, 21st century) talent has continued to widen. This is what I desperately want to change, and what our workforce stats are demanding be changed considering employee engagement and profitability are declining and turnover is skyrocketing. Work isn't working anymore, and if we want to change it for the better, we must start at the top.

## The Need to Lead

Leadership. Make no mistake about it. Leadership really matters. What happens in leadership determines—for better or worse—the quality of life for most people for most of their waking hours. Without leadership, no children are educated, no health services are delivered, no travel happens, no ballet, drama, or movie is presented, no books get published, no science is possible, no firms make money, and no government can be run. Whether you realize it or not, leadership is the biggest single determinant of your quality of life. Leadership is intended to influence and maximize the efforts of others towards the achievement of a goal. Leadership is supposed to add value to an organization, not slow it down or kill initiative.

In the 20th century, leadership was often the equivalent of power, fueled by a top down, "do-it-because-I-said-so" approach to management. It was also a role that had to be earned over time. Few young people were given the opportunity to lead. In its era, this approach to leadership was effective. Here and now, this approach is highly ineffective, even damaging. Consider the following excerpt of an article authored by Uschi Schreiber, Global Vice Chair of Markets and Chair of Global Accounts Committee, following the 2017 World Economic Forum Annual Meeting.

> In the last year especially, we have been confronted with
> an array of grim numbers and escalating events: millions
> of refugees with nowhere to go; unexpected decisions on
> Brexit and in the U.S. elections; melting ice caps; growing
> income and wealth inequality; terrorist atrocities and
> the rise of nationalist and populist politics. ... For much
> of the last century, we expected our leaders to see the
> future, explain the challenges and navigate us through the

contradictions, dilemmas and, of course, the dangers. Most of all, we expected them to work on our behalf to think carefully, critically and strategically to take us safely through the obstacles ahead. Around the world we are now seeing a high level of disillusionment. People have lost confidence in governments and big business and are longing for strong leadership.[1]

Schreiber served up a call to action to leaders worldwide, urging them to create real change without alienating diverse stakeholders, to overcome fear, and to take immediate action as many issues are simultaneously rushing towards a breaking point.

You see, when leadership fails, most of the people are miserable most of the time. That includes the people doing the work, the people for whom the work is done, and the rest of society who are affected by the way the work is done. And right now, we're miserable, and it's largely because our leaders haven't been able to keep pace with the changing needs of our workforce.

We now live in a world in transition; from the model of society we knew for centuries to one that is much more unknown. Businesses in every industry are responding to rapid shifts in the marketplace that would have seemed unimaginable even a few years ago. Smart technology, artificial intelligence, robotics, drones, and driverless cars are on the verge of fundamentally reinventing the workforce and transforming supply chains.

We've moved from the Industrial Era into the Talent Economy and we can't go backward. Our existing framework will come under more and more strain as the world continues to change. The only option is to evolve or to fail.

---

1 Copyright 2017. World Economic Forum. Reprinted with permission from
  https://www.weforum.org/agenda/2017/01/three-big-challenges-for-the-world-in-2017.

## Management vs. Leadership

John Kotter is internationally known as an expert on the topic of leadership. He's the author of 20 books, and Emeritus Professor of Leadership at Harvard Business School. Kotter authored an article in *Harvard Business Review*, "Management Is (Still) Not Leadership," in which he explained the difference between management and leadership.

> ...management is a set of well-known processes, like planning, budgeting, structuring jobs, staffing jobs, measuring performance and problem-solving, which help an organization to predictably do what it knows how to do well. Management helps you to produce products and services as you have promised, of consistent quality, on budget, day after day, week after week. In organizations of any size and complexity, this is an enormously difficult task. We constantly underestimate how complex this task really is, especially if we are not in senior management jobs. So, management is crucial—but it's not leadership.
>
> Leadership is entirely different. It is associated with taking an organization into the future, finding opportunities that are coming at it faster and faster and successfully exploiting those opportunities. Leadership is about vision, about people buying in, about empowerment and, most of all, about producing useful change.[2]

The challenge that exists is that many leaders today excel at management, but not leadership.

Consider the example of Bob, a foreman in a manufacturing company. His job was to organize the work, assign the right people

---

2 Reprinted with permission from January 09, 2013 *Harvard Business Review* Web article, "Management Is (Still) Not Leadership" by John P. Kotter. hbr.org

to the necessary tasks, coordinate the results, and ensure the job got done as ordered. Bob's focus was on efficiency.

Twenty years later, Bob gets a promotion. As the company's new CEO, it's now Bob's job to lead. But in his previous role, he didn't have to give much thought to the company's vision, what he was producing and how, or to the other people who worked for the company. Bob was promoted because he had management experience. He has no idea how to lead, and soon the company begins to struggle.

To Kotter's point, management requires a very different skillset than leadership. Leadership needs to communicate vision, empower, and motivate people, and requires both speed and agility to deal with changing environments. Management needs to forecast, budget, plan, and control.

Here are just a few of the ways management and leadership differ.

| Management | Leadership |
|---|---|
| Administer | Innovate |
| Tell | Inspire |
| Maintain | Develop |
| Systems | People |
| Ask how and when | Ask what and why |
| Focus is on the bottom line | Focus is on the horizon |
| Accept status quo | Challenge status quo |

In the Talent Economy, a manager's duties alone are wholly insufficient for the workplace.

In the Talent Economy, value comes increasingly from the knowledge of people. This is a leadership skill. People look to their leaders not just to assign them a task or maximize efficiency, but to define for them a purpose, nurture their skills, develop their talent and inspire results. In the Talent Economy, if people don't care about the mission, about their leader, or about one another, the team becomes fragmented, disengaged, and eventually falls apart. In the Talent Economy, empathetic, trust-based leadership is the most effective way to lead a team and the most profitable way to run a company.

Kotter wrote,

> There are very, very few organizations today that have sufficient leadership. Until we face this issue, understanding exactly what the problem is, we're never going to solve it. Unless we recognize that we're not talking about management when we speak of leadership, all we will try to do when we do need more leadership is work harder to manage. At a certain point, we end up with over-managed and under-led organizations, which are increasingly vulnerable in a fast-moving world.[1]

## Complacent and Complex

Over-managed and under-led organizations can lead to a worse fate: complacency. Leaders can ignore change to the point of feeling calm and confident even while watching their organizations decline and spiral out of control. Apathy, over-confidence, and the delusion that 'it will change back' prevent leaders from fully comprehending the severity of a talent crisis situation.

Lisa Bodell, CEO of FutureThink, believes complacency stems from complexity. Her team of trainers teach creativity and innovation, and began noticing that although organizational leaders *said* they wanted to think about and plan for the future, what they *did* was quite the opposite.

The FutureThink team would be hired to teach innovation, creativity, and change, but once they started to consult, the organization's leaders would resist. "They'd say 'Color a picture of the future, but keep it within very specific lines, because we want to manage risk'," Bodell explained. "That's ridiculous. That's not what futurists do, that's not what innovators do. That's not going to get them anywhere."

Further research on Bodell's part revealed that these leaders were working in environments that were too complex, and that complexity was making them complacent. "Complacency is where people settle for the status quo. They don't challenge assumptions anymore. They don't come up with new ideas. That's a real problem," she said.

Bodell believes complexity is the outcome of placing experienced managers into leadership roles. Managers are accustomed to administrating and maintaining systems and structures, so when they move into leadership roles they tend to add systems and structures which increases complexity, and that ultimately leads to burnout.

The absence of leadership skills, coupled with the presence of change, has amplified a feeling of fear in many of today's leaders, which can be quite debilitating, resulting in complacency. While drastic failure may catch a leader's attention, it's usually only for the short-term, then there's usually a return to status quo.

## Resisting Change

It's important to understand why some leaders are more likely to resist change than embrace it. In many ways, we've been conditioned to avoid change: either our brains resist it or our leaders are paid to avoid it. Sound crazy? Let's explore each.

For starters, the fear of change prevalent among leaders is a very real and scientifically proven obstacle. When we encounter change, it literally lights up an area of our brain called the prefrontal cortex. The prefrontal cortex is fast and agile. It can store multiple threads of logic at once, enabling us to make computations quickly.

However, the prefrontal cortex's capacity is limited. It can deal comfortably with only a handful of concepts before we max out our capacity. When we reach our limit, we experience a physiological sense of discomfort, usually fatigue or anger towards the change. We experience this because the prefrontal cortex is tightly linked to the emotional center of the brain, the amygdala, which controls our fight-or-flight response. It's like being trained to be a funeral director, then suddenly you're told to be a fighter pilot and you're in a cockpit with enemy planes approaching. A shift like that can feel terrifying!

The prefrontal cortex crashes easily because it burns lots of blood sugar. Given the high-energy cost of running our prefrontal cortex, our brain would rather run off its basal ganglia, which has a much larger storage capacity, storing all our saved memories and the functions we perform most frequently during our daily lives.

Most of the time the basal ganglia is running the show. We rely on our basal ganglia to control most of the repetitive tasks associated with our jobs. Doing what we know hurts less, because its comfortingly predictable. In other words, "doing things the way we've always done them" is preferred because our basal ganglia burns less glucose and causes less discomfort overall.

Simply expecting people to make a change, or even demanding they make a change, is not enough. Our brains resist it, and this becomes more apparent as we age because the older we get, the more our instinct of social conservation kicks in.

We're seeing the desire for social conservation come into play more than ever, likely because many organizations are still operating on Industrial-era methodologies, first incorporated in the late 1700s. (It worked for this long—why wouldn't it work now?) And while change has become the norm, it's harder than ever because we're being expected to change more than ever. This is especially apparent among older generations. Now, more than any other time in their lives, their prefrontal cortexes are on overload, burning more glucose. They're literally feeling burned out by the idea of innovation and change, and they're craving a time when they could just rely on their basal ganglia.

The other reason we're seeing a resistance to change is because our organizations reward leaders for failure. This may sound crazy, but it's true. The late 19th and 20th century approach to leadership was aimed at making money. In its time, that was a sustainable approach. We were building, quite literally, the American Dream: manufacturing more widgets, expanding assembly lines, building bigger buildings, and generating more jobs. The leaders of this era focused on inspiring their employees to work harder to produce more to make more money. Then society decided that the leaders leading their companies to bigger profits should be compensated for those profits. In 1965, executive pay was 24 times that of worker pay. Now it is a whopping 275 times more.

Let's be honest. It's difficult to get leaders to understand and embrace change and take risks, when their salaries depend upon them *not* understanding it. It's not surprising then that leaders will do everything in their power to maintain status quo and wax poetic about things like innovation and change, when really there is no change happening at all.

The monetary influence on change will be addressed in Chapter 4. Money isn't the driving force of the Talent Economy, and we find that history's focus on profits has done considerably more harm than good.

As for the brain's influence on change, there is an antidote: collaboration. Our pre-frontal cortex is closely tied to our fight-or-flight response, but we're less likely to respond with fight or flight when we're supported by, and in community with, other people.

Collaboration would aid us all greatly in easing our fears, making it possible to adapt and accomplish change. We'd likely achieve more and fear less simply by having the option to talk through our fears. We'd be more likely to get out of our comfort zones and take risks because we'd be asking "why?" and "what if?" not as individuals, but as teams. In the process, we'd create workplaces that encourage idea-sharing to successfully change systems, fix processes, work productively, and find solutions. Collaboration helps us manage change and create something valuable out of chaos. There will be more on collaboration in Chapter 6.

First things first: many leaders were trained as managers and lack the skills they need to move organizations forward in the Talent Economy. How can we fix this?

## Leaders for Talent Generation

The worst thing a leader can do is to do nothing. I wish I had a dollar for every time I've heard a CEO say, "It's all good. I don't need to do anything. I'm retiring soon and this will be someone else's problem." These are the coasters; the complacent leaders Kotter refers to who don't have the skills to lead, aren't up to the challenge of leading, then willingly wave the white flag, either too afraid or too lazy to lead. To put it candidly, these are the leaders that are causing employee engagement and productivity to take a nosedive.

The type of leaders we need right now will have a strong sense of passion, humility, and urgency. These are the leadership traits of the Talent Economy. Unlike their 20th-century predecessors, these leaders are visionary, collaborative, and swift, never losing sight of their organization's core purpose or wavering in their desire for change.

### Passion

There are thousands of books written about leadership, but all the knowledge in the world can't make a perfect leader. Often it can come down to caring, passion for the projects, for the organization, and for the people involved. Imagine a leader who has all the right strengths to excel: a top-notch education, knowledge, and great experience. Now imagine this leader, though perhaps excessively equipped to handle the job, has no interest and is disengaged or even cranky at work. His or her heart isn't in it and everyone knows it.

I worked for someone like this early in my career. He'd retreat to his office for hours on end, and when he did make an appearance it was usually to voice a complaint. He seemed to despise his job and his leadership (or lack thereof) cultivated a miserable work environment. In contrast, the people who have a strong passion for what they do radiate a positive energy. Their eyes light up when they talk about their jobs. Passionate leaders are curious and connected. They desire to serve others and want to do the best work possible. They are visionary, and people naturally follow them because they ooze enthusiasm and inspire excellence.

The passionate leaders are the ones who step up and out, helping their organizations take the biggest leaps forward. Leadership passion is a critical trait considering this rapidly changing, uber-competitive 21st-century market we're in. The absence of passion will inevitably lead to employee disengagement and turnover.

Nicole Martin serves as chair of the 101 Best and Brightest Advisory Board in Chicago, an awards program which recognizes companies for exceptional dedication to their employees. Martin said the best organizations—the top 10 percent in Chicago—differ from others simply because the leaders of those organizations care. These leaders don't just say they care, or preach its importance, they are passionate about it and seek to cultivate a culture of caring throughout the entire organization. "If you went into any of the Best and Brightest companies, you would find they are truly entangled with their people—and it starts at the top," Martin said.

Passion is difficult to measure or to teach, but research has proven it's more likely to be present when leaders make dialoguing with their team a priority and practice optimism and positivity. Here are a few trademarks of passionate leaders:

• *Stories*
  Passionate leaders envision the future, and they are able to convey that vision to others. Often, they enthuse others to believe in their cause with attention-getting or inspiring stories. When story-telling is effectively used people become emotionally

involved in new ideas, understanding how they can help
implement a change and willing to go beyond the status quo.

- *Dialogue*
Passionate leaders know they must have faith in others for others
to be passionate about what needs to be accomplished. So they
endorse people as their most valuable assets and empower others
and they make dialoguing with their team and maintaining
relationships a priority.

In 1985, Steven Quick's first job was working as an auditor for a
Fortune 500 company. He clearly remembers the feeling he had as a
young employee. "There was this feeling that the partners of the firm
were like God. They had these large, fancy offices with ornate rugs and
furnishings and most everyone else just had cubicles. They were so
intimidating."

Fast forward 32 years, Quick is now the Chief Executive of Global
Occupier Services at Cushman & Wakefield, a global real estate firm,
having previously held leadership roles at three other companies.
Quick said his early observations of those firm partners influenced
him considerably. He didn't want to project the "shadow of the
leader" or intimidate the people he was leading. "I've seen many
leaders who come at leadership from the approach of being 'large
and in charge' and 'just do what I say.' But this approach doesn't work
and it doesn't motivate." Recognizing this early on, Quick decided to
instead practice servant leadership, which shares power and focuses
on the well-being of others.

So Quick hosts town halls at Cushman & Wakefield in an
effort to be as transparent and as accessible as he possibly can to
30,000 employees. In each town hall, Quick reports on the state of
the organization, the team's priorities, and answers questions from
the employees. "Whatever we do has to resonate with the troops in
order to drive a positive culture," he explained. "Leadership starts at

the top, but it has to be a groundswell to be effective." Quick said he is always encouraging his team to help one another, motivate, coach, and develop one another towards greater success. "Our asset is our people. If we fail or falter in the caring of our greatest assets, we'll see consolidation or decline," he said.

Benjamin Rashleger is president and CEO at WSI Industries, a precision manufacturing company for the aerospace, defense, medical, and energy markets. When he was 35 years old, he was named CEO, replacing a retiring CEO who had been at WSI for several years. Despite growing up in a family business, starting work at the age of 12, and managing people older than him in previous roles, being a young CEO proved challenging; all of Rashleger's direct reports are at least 10 years older than he is.

Given the circumstances, Rashleger said he is always careful to think about his audience. "Many leaders think about how they want to be heard, but not interpreted. Leadership requires pause, reflection, and thinking about others," he said. "I'm always expressing my opinion in a way that's respectful and I'm very careful to always think about my audience."

- *Positivity*
  Negative energy kills passion. When you get a call from someone who complains and drains your energy, this leads to distraction and that distraction leads us to being ineffective. Passionate leaders try to stay positive. They do things that energize them and surround themselves with other passionate, knowledgeable experts who will guide them with ideas and honest feedback.

While you can't accurately measure passion, researchers have found that leaders who worked towards their organizational goals with intensity and genuine excitement were more successful overall. These leaders are more likely to believe they have control over their futures, which means they aren't derailed by daily challenges and they counteract their frustrations by focusing on what is going right.

Recently I have witnessed a high level of frustration from leaders who just seem to be burned out. They are worn out, overwhelmed, and frustrated, which isn't surprising considering the current rate of change. However, it's imperative we find the passionate leaders and do what we can to hone this attribute in all our leaders. Passion is critical to talent generation. It keeps leaders personally invested in the success of their organizations and motivates them to nurture the mission—and the people working there—with enthusiasm and conviction.

## Humility

This conflicts with the conventional 20th century view of the chief executive as a wildly independent and often egotistic commander. In fact, it would seem that during a time of incredible disruption, society would want and need commanding leaders, directing everything and everyone with masterful insight. Yet, the opposite has proven true. The fact is, the pace of change has ensured that no one is an expert, and for the first time in history, every generation has something to learn and something to teach. As Ken Blanchard, the 77-year-old management expert and author of more than 60 books, put so eloquently: None of us is smarter than all of us. Never before has this statement been more accurate.

The best leaders of today are self-aware enough to know that they can't possibly know or do everything, and they aren't afraid to turn to advisors and employees to seek new ideas and points of view. They are constantly in pursuit of the best new ideas, and they don't care if those ideas come from themselves or from someone else.

The best leaders are not content to operate solely on what they currently know. They recognize that the demands of their position are always changing, and they need to better themselves to keep their organizations successful. As a result, they possess an incredible desire to always be absorbing new information, honing new skills, and bettering their own abilities through constant learning. This learning isn't limited to books and podcasts, but actually immersing oneself into dialogue and experiences with younger people. It's this consistent intellectual immersion that keeps leaders on their toes, forcing them to re-evaluate, defend, and question what they know.

As a consultant, I often advise the leaders I work with to spend time engaged in conversation with younger people. I've learned that the most successful, visionary leaders are already doing this as a regular practice, whereas the leaders of organizations that are struggling to survive spend little to no time with people in age groups other than their own. This is also true of most boards of directors, which tend to be largely composed of executives with experience. But experience simply isn't enough to keep an organization afloat in the 21st century.

### 30-30-30

During the next 30 days, hold 30 conversations with 30 people under the age of 30. Ask them the following questions:

- What is challenging for people in your age group right now?

- Think of an experience when you felt like you really belonged. What did the organization do or the experience provide to make you feel that way?

- What one word would you use to describe success?

Note what you learn from this exercise. Even better if you do this with a team and share your findings as a group. Ask: Is our organization equipped to meet the needs of the next generation? Why or why not?

True humility, scientists have learned, is when leaders have an accurate assessment of both their strengths and weaknesses, and see all this in the context of the larger whole. Humility is understanding that you are part of something far greater than yourself. Humility is a balance of recognizing your abilities as well as your flaws. It's knowing where you can contribute, and where you need to improve or grow.

Humility's benefits are surprisingly concrete. Several sources including *The Washington Post* have reported on a study by researchers from Duke University that explored the differences between humility and arrogance in the workforce in detail. Here are a few examples of how the researchers define the differences between the intellectually humble and intellectually arrogant:

| Intellectually Arrogant | Intellectually Humble |
| --- | --- |
| Rarely change their minds | Will change their views with new evidence |
| Seek to place blame | Seek to build connections |
| Don't like asking for help | Willing to ask for help |
| Has all the answers, never makes mistakes | Admits mistakes and limitations |

Intellectually arrogant leaders get their strength from a position of certainty, concentrating on power. They remove others with strong abilities, perceiving them to be a threat. They alone get credit for success, and never make mistakes. (Someone else is to blame.) Followers carry out edicts rather than contribute new insight.

Research proves this approach is less effective:

- According to a *Journal of Management* study of 105 technology firms, humble CEOs dispersed their power, hired more diverse management teams, gave staff the ability to lead and innovate, and had a reduced pay disparity between themselves and their staff.

- University of California research proved that intellectually humble college students perform higher in academic
  achievement, improve more over the course of a semester, and
  get better grades.
- A global Catalyst study revealed that humble leaders have higher
  employee satisfaction, less employee turnover, and improve the
  company's overall performance.

Keep in mind, both arrogance and humility are contagious. Both
can be taught and caught. That's why you may hear someone refer
to a "toxic culture" at work, or by contrast, hear someone rave about
how much they love going to work. Workplace culture is determined
by leadership. Leaders are creating an environment where workers
either feel appreciated or overlooked; inspired to innovate or fearful of
change; collaborative or egotistic.

David Dyjack worked in 70 countries as a public health scientist
before moving into leadership roles. He realizes his track to leadership
wasn't typical, and his early career's focus on service made a lasting
impression on him. Since he was named executive director and CEO
of the National Environmental Health Association (NEHA) in 2015,
Dyjack has taken an unconventional approach to leadership.

Dyjack referred to NEHA at the time of his onboarding as "a great
place to work but not a family." Bringing his years of public health
into his leadership style, Dyjack leads from the perspective that
successful organizations have employees who are capable of loving
and respecting one another. "The concept of love in organizations is
undervalued. But when people feel loved, they are less likely to get
sick," he said, explaining the health of an organization relies on how
the people who work there are feeling.

To create this sense of family, Dyjack started by asking his team,
"Why aren't you failing more?" The topic of failure became a regular
part of NEHA's discussions and team meetings. Normalizing failure

empowered employees and created a learning environment at NEHA. "I tell people that 95 out of 100 new things we try won't work, but we learn more from failure than from not trying. I also tell them that when you fail, I'll be here to catch you and pick you up," Dyjack said. Establishing an environment where failure is acceptable has led to more collaboration, trust, and cooperation.

Dyjack practices what he preaches. "I'm trying many things to inspire and make this an aspirational place to work," he said. This has included the launch of the "best retirement plan," alternate work schedules in summer, closing the office for a week during the holidays, and a corporate wellness program which includes yoga sessions on-site.

Moreover, Dyjack has pushed the team to question the relevance of everything at NEHA. As he put it, NEHA had to stop operating on "auto-pilot." While the organization was doing well, Dyjack had a bigger vision in mind. "I want this to be the most influential health organization on the planet and we will do this through relationships," he said. These relationships have included extending event invitations to organizations once considered competitors, a decision for which Dyjack has fallen under criticism.

"I'm not Mr. Popular. I'm taking a lot of hits right now," he said, referring to the pushback on some of his leadership decisions. But Dyjack has held steadfast to his value for relationship-building. He believes the future of the industry will be better by forging alliances, rather than working in a silo and waging war on other organizations. Nevertheless, in the spirit of relationship-building, Dyjack said he values the "curmudgeons and contrarians because they challenge me."

Dyjack's quest for relevance and growth includes a think-tank of young professionals, which he organized on his own and calls on frequently for feedback. Dyjack said being a leader means accepting that you don't have all the answers, and that there are times when you should lead, and times when you should follow. He knew he had to be forward-thinking in his decisions and seek an outside, unjaded, and honest perspective from people who were much younger than himself. "Some of the best ideas have come from this under 30 group," he said.

Dyjack's quest has also included risk assessment. Prior to making any change, he assesses the benefits and the potential losses. "Anytime change happens, you have to know what you stand to lose." Dyjack said he often had to choose between loyalty and vision. In the end, he was willing to lose some of NEHA's loyal members to stay true to his vision of creating the most influential health organization on the planet.

So far, the risk has been worth the reward. One year after Dyjack took the helm, NEHA's membership had increased 20 percent, reported the best financial year in the organization's history, and attendance at the annual president's banquet grew by 166 percent. (Attendees didn't want to leave the banquet. Police actually came in to shut it down—a point of pride that Dyjack doesn't mind sharing.) But Dyjack is quick to point out that success is not a reason to sit back and celebrate. "Leadership is fatiguing," he said, but without consistent effort and focus on NEHA's vision, he's afraid the association will return to auto-pilot or adopt a normalcy bias, failing to adapt during a time of tremendous change and opportunity.

So the CEO of NEHA remains focused on relationship-building in the industry, among the membership, and within its team of 40 people. "We're a nonprofit. We can't provide the top salary but we can offer top benefits and working conditions. Individuals who work here want to be associated with success and inclusivity, to be part of a social fabric that's exciting. We provide that. We provide dynamic, changing, and challenging conditions. We will not be static—and that's what made the difference." It isn't the practice of tearing others down that pushes us to work to become our best selves. It's humility.

## Urgency

Researchers found that urgency often manifested in successful CEOs as impatience is really a consistent eagerness to drive progress. Most quality leaders are experts at mobilizing their teams, but the very best leaders are driven by a constant and deeply personal need to move things forward and seek new developments. They aren't satisfied with moving slowly or with too much caution. They understand the importance of staying nimble and pushing their organizations towards transformative change. It's important to note, however, that the best leaders don't just make unreasonably impulsive decisions; they take measured risks to move their organizations into the future and keep ahead of the competition.

The unfortunate reality is that many leaders aren't functioning under the umbrella of urgency, which was the point of Uschi Schreiber's World Economic Forum speech mentioned earlier in the chapter. She served up a call to action to leaders worldwide, urging them to take immediate action. Now is the time to lead, to prioritize talent generation, and to pass the baton. No organization can afford to wait.

## Pass the Baton Already

A couple years ago I met the senior HR manager of a medical manufacturing company over coffee. Exasperated, she told me the company was on the brink of crisis, preparing to lose about 60 percent of its workforce within the next five years. I assumed this meant the company needed to ramp up its efforts to recruit younger workers. Turns out the "crisis" existed at the top. "Recruiting isn't the problem. The problem is getting our leaders to work with our younger people and help train them." Further explanation revealed that company-wide, only a few of the employees on the verge of retirement had agreed to fulfill the company's request to spend time with their younger co-workers, allowing them to either interview or job-shadow them for the purposes of training and that essential art of baton-passing.

"I've never seen anything like it," the HR manager told me. "There's this widespread apathy among senior leaders. Many of them have worked here for 30 years or more, and now that they're on the way out, they don't care about the future of the company. They are purposely avoiding any efforts to collaborate or even interact with our next generation of leaders. It's like they feel entitled. They're actually saying, 'I had to learn this on my own, now you will have to do the same.' And after this company provided them with a great job and great benefits for 30 years, they don't care whether the company sinks or swims." Meanwhile, the company's middle management is feeling panicked and stuck—so stuck they are seriously considering offering the retirees part-time consulting opportunities.

This situation is a perfect example of what Kotter referred to as complacent leadership. In the absence of leadership skills or the presence of change, fear is amplified and complacency takes over. It seems more appealing to ignore and avoid anything (and anyone) that represents the fear associated with change. This is an epic failure on many levels.

Millennials are the largest generation in history, becoming the workforce majority in 2015. Harnessing the talent and loyalty of this generational cohort is absolutely critical as many of these Millennials ascend to leadership positions. Deloitte estimates that Millennials will make up 75 percent of the global workforce by 2025. However, the leadership development of Millennials has not yet been considered a priority.

Despite substantial efforts by learning professionals, a multi-billion dollar leadership development industry, and more than 70 years of leadership research, the overall success by organizations to grow leaders remains dismal. Consider the following.

- The Brandon Hall Group's 2015 State of Leadership Development Study found that just 20 percent of organizations identified the Millennial leader segment as critical for development over the next 24 months.

- Deloitte interviewed more than 2,000 global HR and business leaders in 2016, and discovered only 25 percent of these were building talent in their organizations. (This is despite the fact that organizations' efforts and spending on leadership development was increasing every year.)

- According to the 2016 Deloitte Millennial Survey, which surveyed nearly 7,700 Millennials in 29 countries, 63 percent of Millennials said their leadership skills are not being fully developed. The survey also found that those Millennials intending to stay with their organization for more than five years are twice as likely to have a mentor (68 percent), than not (32 percent).

- The Hartford's Millennial Leadership Survey found that the number one thing employers can do to demonstrate their investment in a young person becoming a leader is to train and develop them, including coaching and mentoring.

There's a common theme here. Clearly, most organizations aren't invested in the coaching and mentoring of Millennials, yet Millennials want and need leadership development.

Attracting and retaining the best of this generation is critical to the future of any business. While the Millennial population in the workforce is increasing rapidly, many Baby Boomers have already reached, or are fast approaching, retirement age.

The average age of CEOs in the S&P 500 Index rose by 4 percent from 55.2 in 2006 to 57.2 in 2016. A separate analysis of America's top 1,000 companies by revenue put the average CEO age at 58. When global stock markets collapsed in 2008, there was a high turnover rate of CEOs aged 64 and above. But since markets have improved, elder CEOs have come back into favor, making talent generation and planning for the future even more important. The forthcoming loss of skills and experience built up over many years will leave a significant skills gap in the not-too-distant future.

If anything, Millennials are the best-placed generation to develop as leaders because of their understanding of the reality of today's world. They came of age in the Talent Economy. Their skillsets and worldviews are unique and valuable. While each business will require a unique strategy to fit their leadership needs, there are effective practices that should be commonplace. Mentorship is one of these practices.

## Mentoring

As one might imagine, it is difficult to recruit employees to a home remodeling company. But in 2015, Power Home Remodeling of Chester, Penn., garnered the highest scores in Great Place to Work's survey of workers under the age of 35, landing the number one spot on the inaugural list of 100 Best Workplaces for Millennials. (That means it beat out Google.)

Power focuses on empowering its 1,500 employees and creating opportunities for advancement, and places a strong emphasis on mentorship in the company. Power's mentorship program starts on day one. Each new hire is assigned a personal mentor to provide guidance, support, and encouragement. Also, every position in every department at Power has a blueprint designed to guide, support, and challenge employees to achieve more through mentorship and management opportunities.

In addition, the senior leaders at Power host quarterly leadership conferences at various destinations throughout the country with the objective of bringing a few hundred of the company's future leaders together to share insight into expansion plans, new product launches, recruitment objectives, and general operations.

Interestingly enough, both the co-CEOs at Power Home Remodeling are Millennials, and so is 84 percent of the staff, whose average age is 29 years old.

Millennials are typically more interested than previous generations in finding a mentor. They have grown up with the notion that one must constantly seek the advice of another, and social media has put this notion on steroids. Millennials live in a world where once you post a picture of a potential purchase on Instagram, which then gets copied to your Twitter feed and Facebook page, advice and comments flood in within seconds.

Millennials believe—because they were taught this from a young age—that their ideas are important and valuable. They crave—because they had access from a young age—opportunities to learn. This passion for lifelong learning is a tremendous strength. However, mentoring doesn't look the same as it has traditionally. (Have Millennials ever taken a traditional approach to anything?)

Millennials don't need traditional classroom-based leadership training. They don't want to spend time studying. In their time-pressed world, they are eager to get to action. They will respond much better to approaches that allow them to practice and ritualize new leadership behaviors without leaving the context of day-to-day life.

Also, Millennials don't rely on one mentor. After all, they are active in many different forums, like LinkedIn, which provides immediate access to industry professionals from around the world. In the Talent Economy, one senior person can no longer be the only place a young person turns for career support.

In the Talent Economy, mentoring programs aren't hierarchical or time-consuming. Senior leaders have invaluable knowledge that demands to be shared, but so do Millennials. Every generation has something to learn and something to teach, which is where reverse mentoring comes in.

**Reverse Mentoring**

Reverse mentoring is an initiative where older executives are mentored by younger employees on topics like technology, social media, and current trends. Yes, Millennials mentoring executives. This trend has a double-sided benefit. Executives stay on the pulse of trends that are most important to the elusive Millennial, while the younger participant feels more connected and invested because they are contributing to the improvement of their company at the highest level.

IBM's Millennial Corps is a digital group of thousands of young employees who converse on their own internal platform, as well as attend local events. Millennial Corps members tend to be the "beta testers" and "intrapreneurs" fostering a startup-like culture within the company.

The whole project started out rather informally when four IBM employees were asked by senior executives about ways they could change how younger employees engage and positively influence the company. These employees decided to survey other young IBM employees to see what they most wanted from the company. While answers varied, two things stood out: young employees wanted to be able to work on projects they were passionate about and they liked the idea of having a direct pipeline to the top decision makers.

Since then, Millennial Corps has ballooned in size to more than 5,000 people. It consists of a self-selecting group of IBM employees who consider themselves part of the younger generation. Membership happened organically—generally through word of mouth from other members—and it's become an international group with over 65 countries represented.

Millennial Corps members connect via IBM's own digital platform, allowing them to chat with each other. They also frequently receive surveys about potential projects IBM may be spearheading. When IBM is preparing to launch a new product, the Millennials Corps tests it out, providing feedback on what's working, what isn't, and if any design fixes need to be made.

But there's another dimension, too. The Millennial Corps is a way for Millennials to feel connected with the hundreds of thousands of their co-workers at IBM. With 377,000 employees in more than 170 countries, IBM is a massive organization. Millennial Corps has proven effective at establishing a community, as well as a mechanism for feedback and relevance. IBM has positioned itself as "a legacy company learning how to remain relevant." The Millennial Corps is helping IBM find ways to remain agile and disprove the theory that only startup companies can innovate.

The Millennial Corps feedback has impacted many of IBM's recent decisions, according to a report in *Fast Company*. Millennial Corps ambassadors have met with the executive team, including CEO Ginni Rometty. IBM seems to be learning from the younger generation and heeding their advice, which is the first step to collaboration, relationship-building, engagement, and belonging.

In a similar vein, Target reportedly contracts with Techstars, a company which partners tech startups with large corporations to help fast-track their growth. But Target reversed the process, asking members of the Techstars' team to teach Target executives best practices from the start-up world. Target reportedly wants its executives to learn from the way start-ups work—working quickly and scrappily to get things done.

UnitedHealth Group rolled out a reverse mentoring program in 2016 which paired eight senior executives in its insurance division with eight Millennials seen as emerging leaders from their health IT division. The average age gap between the executives and emerging leaders is 25 years. The fact is, UnitedHealth's insurance business is perceived as less innovative than its fast-growing health IT division, Optum. The reverse mentoring program serves to help the insurance executives see the business with fresh eyes and shape a workplace that reflects the contrasting needs of the next generation. Via reverse mentoring, young professionals become more confident and gain valuable skills as they learn to "coach" their older colleagues.

On the flipside, the exchange equips experienced leaders with fresh approaches by seeing how younger, diverse employees solve problems and view current trends within their respective industry. Reverse mentoring also gives organizations a competitive advantage because the experienced leaders hear from the Millennials themselves how to target them as employees and consumers and potentially win over this largest share of the market.

### Micro-Mentoring

Another form of mentorship is micro-mentoring. This is the use of casual, informal meetings or interactions. The rise of social media has driven up the use of micro-mentoring. There are even apps, like Rungway, and platforms, like MicroMentor, dedicated to micro-mentoring communities.

The micro method diverges from the traditional one-on-one approach to mentoring, aiming to be less formal and shorter term than other mentoring programs. Micro-mentoring allows professionals to have many mentors for brief periods of time and is usually designed to help professionals improve a very specific skill, such as time management.

BMO Financial and its BMO Harris Bank unit launched a micro-mentoring program for its female employees in late 2016, growing out of employees' requests for quick access to skill-building opportunities rather than going through formal training. Those interested in being mentors can sign up through BMO Financial's intranet and list their specific skill sets. Participants can simply search the intranet for mentors who are experts in the area they are interested in working on.

Intel runs a long-standing program that matches employees with mentors (in-person or virtual) based on the skills and interests of the mentee. Participants must fill out a questionnaire, which then is used to match them with other qualifying employees who can teach them the skills they desire to learn.

As the business landscape continues to experience a seismic shift in operations and deliverability, we need to mold a generation of leaders who can effectively adapt. It is key to future growth and success. Across every industry, trends like globalization, digitalization, and consumerization are changing the way our executives interact and overcome business challenges. Training Millennials for these leadership roles must be a proactive process, or else companies risk being left behind.

Boomers and Generation Xers need to be willing mentors for Millennials, and need to be open to opportunities for Millennials to mentor them. It is not a question of volunteering. It is a matter of talent generation by providing feedback, encouraging and inspiring others, and demonstrating the characteristics of a strong leader.

Support, encouragement, and regular feedback are all essential in molding a generation of future leaders. Understanding their ambitions and welcoming their ideas will also go far in developing individuals who are not only ready to take on executive roles, but also who are loyal to your organization.

## Avoiding a Kodak Moment

Getting back to the hoodie. On the day of Facebook's IPO in 2012, Mark Zuckerberg was harshly criticized for being unprepared, immature, and destined to fail. At the time this book is being written, Facebook is worth $328 billion and Zuckerberg, now 32, is worth $54.9 billion. In 2016, CNN Money reported that analysts are predicting Facebook's profits will grow 32 percent annually, on average, for the next few years—twice the expected earnings growth rate for Google and nearly triple Apple's estimated growth rate.

It wasn't revealed until after the IPO that Zuckerberg had mentors. The Facebook CEO would later share in an interview that when he hit a rough patch in the early days of Facebook, Steve Jobs, co-founder, chairman, and CEO of Apple Inc., mentored him and gave him some great advice. Since 2005, Zuckerberg has also been mentored by Don Graham, CEO of the Washington Post Company.

Could Zuckerberg have been as successful without the guidance of Jobs and Graham? Possibly. But there's no doubt that Zuckerberg learned a lot from his mentors and applied some of their wisdom to his own business practices. Without their involvement, the outcome could have been quite different. For example, Graham advised Zuckerberg to hire COO Sheryl Sandberg and encouraged Sandberg to accept the position, even though she'd be reporting to someone younger. His relationship with Graham formed a template Zuckerberg would rely on in seeking mentorship. Today, his roster of mentors includes Bill Gates, co-founder of Microsoft, and Marc Andreessen, co-creator of the Mosaic internet browser. Graham, today a director of Facebook's board, benefited from his relationship with Zuckerberg too, learning from him about online initiatives that would engage *Washington Post* readers.

When they met in 2005, Graham was 60 years old and Zuckerberg was 21. Graham offered to invest $6 million in Facebook. Zuckerberg accepted, only to renege when another entity offered to invest at a higher valuation. Yet Graham, rather than feeling snubbed, was impressed with how Zuckerberg handled the situation. Later that year, Zuckerberg shadowed Graham for several days.

It was probable that Graham wouldn't have given Zuckerberg a second thought. Be it biology, lack of training or passion or humility, the struggle to transition from the Industrial Era to the Talent Economy is real. As a result, too many of today's experienced leaders are opting out, disinterested in investing in the next generation of leaders.

In my current role, I'm a consultant to organizations struggling to engage younger generations. One recent conversation I had took place with the executive of a large healthcare organization who told me: "We have a saying in our company that's harsh but true. The saying is this: We eat our young. It means that we treat our young staff badly; so badly that they leave within a short period of time. We realize we're doing it, we know it's wrong, but we just can't seem to stop ourselves." We eat our young. Think that's unusual? It's not. The fact is, leaders over the age of 45 were raised in a workforce environment that trained them to believe that younger generations aren't worthy of power or opportunity.

Actually, hierarchy is a practice that dates back to caveman days. The eldest person in any society has the most experience, and therefore has the most wisdom, and therefore should hold the most power. Younger people have little to no influence in a hierarchy because it is believed they lack the necessary skills and expertise.

But for the first time in history, largely due to advancements in education and technology, every generation has something to learn and something to teach. For the first time in history, we're realizing businesses and communities are more powerful when they collaborate and bring a broad range of skills and talent to the table, regardless of age.

Of course, this is easier said than done. The leader of a national organization recently described the onboarding of younger leaders to me as a tremendous risk, even though the organization is seeing the worst revenues and turnover in many years. The organization is failing, and still it seems too risky to invite young people into leadership? Is it not a greater risk to stand still, do nothing, and face imminent demise?

Take Kodak for instance. In 1976, Kodak had 89 percent market share of film sales in the United States. A few decades later, the Kodak name became synonymous with a resistance to change, for its slowness in transitioning to digital photography. In 2012, the company filed for bankruptcy.

But there's another side to their story. In 2011, Kodak placed second on the list of Top 10 *Fortune* 500 Employers With Older Workers. With 38 percent of its workforce over the age of 50, the company was singled out for employing an unusually high percentage of mature workers. I can't help but wonder: If Kodak had paid attention to its aging workforce trend and focused on bringing in younger talent sooner, would the company have maintained market share and avoided bankruptcy? I believe so. Imagine how much more relevant and successful our entities could be, simply by bringing experienced leaders into community and collaboration with young professionals.

Leadership is intended to influence and maximize the efforts of others. Leadership is supposed to add value to an organization. Leadership shouldn't be standing at the ready to point out a young person's mistakes, question their abilities, tell them they're immature, or as in Zuckerberg's case, go so far as to suggest a job change and call them a villain and thief. Thus far, Mark Zuckerberg has succeeded at building a billion-dollar business capable of changing the world. That's the leadership we need right now—with or without the hoodie.

## CHAPTER SUMMARY

In the 20th century organizations were built for efficiency. Most innovation was driven from within the company's four walls, and leadership was reserved for those with the most experience. Many organizations today are structured in such a way that they still consider experience the sole advantage.

In this 21st century Talent Economy, a chasm occurs when experience is perceived to be the sole advantage and organizations avoid the adoption of new ideas, strategies, and approaches. The gap between executive-level (experienced, 20th century) and entry-level (innovative, 21st century) talent has continued to widen. As a result, employee engagement and profitability are declining and turnover is skyrocketing.

Until our leaders shift their focus from management practices rooted in hierarchy onto collaboration and innovation with young professionals, we will continue to observe widespread skills and knowledge gaps which will likely lead to business closings, decreased competitiveness, and economic decline.

## QUESTIONS TO CONSIDER

1. What may be different about your generation's management style and expectations in the workplace in comparison to other generations?

2. What do employees need and expect from you?

3. What skills could you learn from others?

4. How much time do you spend:
   - Advocating on behalf of younger generations?
   - Listening to people in different age groups?
   - Thinking about the future?

5. How much time does the organization spend on the above activities?

6. What three steps will you take in the next 30 days to improve your leadership or team-building efforts?

*In Chapter 2, we started at the top with leadership. As leadership begins to shift focus from management practices rooted in hierarchy onto collaboration with young professionals, it's critical to bridge the generation gaps and employee engagement gaps plaguing your organization. Therefore, Chapter 3 delves into acceptance, inclusion, and trust.*

Build the Future
Education and Business Align

Leadership
Passion, Optimism, Humility, Urgency

Collaborate
Innovation via Team-Building

Acceptance
Inclusion and Trust

Future Focus
Research, Trends, Opportunities

People First
Mission, Vision, and Strategy

*"When the safe path proves to be more treacherous than anyone could have imagined, who can blame us for going our own way, wherever that might lead?"*

NADIRA HIRA

. . . . . . . . . . . . . . . . . . . . . . . . . . . .

## CHAPTER 3

# Acceptance

Jackie Safier is on a mission to revolutionize the apartment business. This quest is obvious just from looking at the company's website, which states "At Prometheus, you're not a resident; you're a neighbor." In fact, when you make the decision to live in a Prometheus Neighborhood, you'll receive the Ultimate Neighbor Experience™, which includes access to the loaner toolbox named Blue, a welcome kit full of toys and treats for your pets, and the opportunity to volunteer or donate to the Promethean Outreach and Community Help program (POrCH).

As one might expect from the company's unique branding to their "neighbors," Prometheus delivers an exceptionally unique and successful employee culture. Millennials comprise an estimated 60 percent of Prometheus' workforce and the average employee tenure is six-and-a-half years, considerably longer than the national two-year average for employee tenure among this age group.

Hearing about Prometheus makes it sound a lot like a start-up company, but it's not. The company was founded by Safier's father in 1965, and Prometheus has managed to continually innovate, adapt, grow, and prosper. Today, Prometheus Real Estate Group is the largest private owner of multi-family properties in the San Francisco Bay Area. Since Safier took over as president in 1992, Prometheus has racked up more than 75 awards, including Best Property Management Firm in the United States. How has a 52-year-old apartment rental company managed to stay relevant? By investing in its people.

Above all, Safier seeks to work with other revolutionaries like herself. "Anyone who wants to work with us has to have the propensity for change. We're very clear that we're setting out to revolutionize the industry and that we're looking for people who are interested in doing the same." she explained.

"Prometheans" as Safier refers to them, are encouraged to refer the people they know for job openings; friends or contacts who would likely resemble the company's entrepreneurial spirit and pride. In fact, 50 percent of Prometheus employees have been referred by other Prometheans. Prometheus creates printed invitations and employees are empowered to hand out these invitations to people they meet who would be a good fit for the company. Safier said a company should never just rely on the human resources department to recruit, because the best hires are usually referrals.

Prometheus has maintained its award-winning status by going above-and-beyond to create a great workplace. "We put forth a lot of effort to build our community," she said. The community-building isn't only good for employee culture, but helps Prometheus maintain its cutting-edge competitiveness by providing an endless stream of new ideas.

Once a month, Safier hosts a roundtable, inviting in a cross-section of 10 employees to meet with her. "Coffee with the president is an opportunity for me to get feedback from the team and I respond to every single suggestion," she said. "Culturally, this is really impactful."

Prometheus also has its own think tank composed of a mix of people representing Prometheus employees and professionals from the field of property acquisition, development, and management. But this think tank is anything but typical. Just about anyone would be honored and elated to serve, considering the unique experience Prometheus provides.

Safier explained think tank participants essentially receive the equivalent of an MBA in marketing over the course of the year, studying from the best brands in the world and making recommendations on how Prometheus can engage and empower their "neighbors" and employees. "We've flown our think tank on Virgin Airlines, shopped for cars with them, and put them up for a night at the Four Seasons," Safier said.

The think tank is hand-picked, then meets once a month for a year. Upon graduation from the think tank, participants are asked to pick someone to take their place and serve on the following year's think tank. Prometheus maintains its relationship with think tank alums, hosting an alumni lunch once a quarter.

"The apartment industry is a service business. It is so important, but so behind," Safier said. "Plus, we're competing for talent with many other companies in Silicon Valley. If we want to stay relevant and competitive and engage great talent, we have to continually build relationships and generate new ideas."

## The Capacity to Change

Over the last 15 years or so, a lot of employee engagement research has been done. People and companies have thrown a great deal of money at the problem of disengagement and turnover and there are likely hundreds of thousands of articles and thought pieces written on the topic. And yet, according to Gallup, the number of actively engaged employees in the United States has averaged less than 33 percent over the past decade.

I think we can all agree that the level at which a business can engage its employees is what determines its success. Yet, the numbers are telling. Despite all the research and writings and contemplation that's been done, we're flunking employee engagement.

As I explained in Chapter 1, employee engagement and profitability have been markedly declining nationwide since 1965. Ironically, 1965 is the same year Prometheus Real Estate Group was founded. That company hasn't observed decline. Quite the opposite has happened, in fact.

Yes, Safier has dedicated herself to the pursuit of revolutionizing the industry and ensuring the success of her organization. And in the last chapter, the critical role leadership plays in the destiny of every organization is explored in greater detail. But the widespread failure to engage employees warrants further exploration. There are several myths and misunderstandings as to what drives employee engagement and how to achieve it. Consider the following common misperceptions.

## Myth: Employee engagement happens naturally

Motivosity, a peer recognition software company, surveyed 357 leaders of the Inc. 5000 list and found that 98 percent of CEOs only look at annual employee engagement surveys once a year and don't discuss engagement with their employees. This may have worked in the Industrial Era, but it certainly doesn't work now.

It's called the Talent Economy for a reason. Talent is driving today's economy, which means talent must be the priority. Employee engagement doesn't just happen and it isn't a one-and-done process. It isn't a program or initiative of the business; it *is* the business. Relationship-building must begin on day one of an employee's job, and be a continual effort.

Companies that understand the importance of employee engagement go beyond the annual engagement survey or company picnic: they re-design jobs, change the work environment, add new benefits, continuously develop managers, and invest in their people.

## Myth: Employee engagement is an HR effort

The Motivosity Inc 5000 survey further indicated that 70 percent of CEOs surveyed delegated culture and engagement problems to the HR department. Here again, in the Industrial Era this made perfect sense. In the Talent Economy, it makes no sense.

Employee engagement is the outcome of building an organization that is exciting, fulfilling, meaningful, and fun. It takes the involvement of engaged leaders, committed to an organization's long-term success, to make talent the priority throughout the entire organization. When employee engagement sits solely in the HR department, the HR team will inevitably realize the challenges associated with talent, then will be forced to navigate the channels of the organization to get buy-in and approval for changes. This process delays and complicates the situation, and sooner or later the HR team gets frustrated, morale plummets, and the people who are supposed to be engaging your talent are feeling especially disengaged. It's a recipe for disaster.

I've seen it happen firsthand. One of my former clients was a global consumer product company. Retention was high among the Boomer generation, but the company was struggling to engage younger talent. Turnover was quite high, as was tension and conflict. The HR department was charged with fixing the problem, but it was obvious that would be a nearly impossible feat. Here's why: The executive team was uninvolved and largely unaware of the company's talent troubles. As a result, they were resistant to the idea of change and severely limited the opportunities for younger people to be promoted, share their opinions, or engage. Nearly every solution the HR department proposed to the executive team was shot down.

I ran into the HR executive for the U.S. division recently. She told me she had left her former company after 12 years because she was sick of being on a ship that the executive team refused to save from sinking.

If you want to increase employee engagement, you have to actually engage one another. This means removing the silos that prohibit your organization from approaching talent development and relationship-building efforts as a team.

Take a lesson from Joshua Reeves, the CEO of Gusto, a human resources software company. As the company quickly scaled to 350 employees and Reeves delegated more tasks to more people, he soon came to the realization he didn't understand what his people did on a granular level. So the CEO made the admirable decision to shadow one person in each of the 37 teams that make up Gusto. From product design to software engineering to social media, Reeves made the effort to spend 60–90 minutes shadowing someone each week. He even spent time greeting the company's guests at the reception desk.

While Reeves' story is encouraging, I highly doubt many CEOs have followed his path of shadowing their company's employees. They may make their rounds in visiting employees in their various locations, but how many of them spend a few hours learning the finer points of what goes into their day-to-day jobs?

There is a level of detachment that I think every leader faces, and this detachment was expected, even encouraged in the Industrial Era. But in the Talent Economy, relationships are crucial. It's important for executives and managers to ensure they fully understand what it's like to work for their company.

## Myth: Millennials are impossible to engage

Employee turnover is costing our nation's organizations an estimated $30.5 billion annually, and this turnover is most acute among younger generations. I've heard every excuse in the book for why this is happening: Millennials have no concept of loyalty, want constant feedback, want everything online, don't value experience, have no work ethic, aren't reliable. They're demanding, annoying, and lazy. Or perhaps you've heard it said another way: our industry isn't "cool" anymore, or "we just can't compete with those tech start-ups."

Let me be clear: your organization's inability to engage talent has very little to do with outside forces. It comes down to *you* and the other people working with you; either you are creating an environment that engages people or you're not. Either your organization is evolving or it's not.

If your organization is struggling to engage talent, look within. Stop making excuses and blaming others. It's not someone else's fault, it's yours. If your organization is struggling to engage talent, it's likely because the way your organization treats its talent isn't engaging or relevant.

This makes me think of the time I met with the leadership of a consulting company that does a lot of work with government entities. The leaders were lamenting the loss of young talent to tech start-ups. For over an hour I listened to them prattle on about everything that was wrong with the company: too old-fashioned, moved too slow, paid too little, too many cubicles, and on and on.

When I asked the leaders to tell me all the reasons why a Millennial would want to work for them, suddenly there was nothing to say. When they finally did respond, it was to say the company was one of the largest and oldest companies in their field.

First of all, in the Talent Economy, the fact that your organization was founded 100 years ago or makes a billion dollars a year means nothing. Legacies don't engage talent, people do.

Second, employee engagement is the reflection of an organization's community. In this case, it was obvious the leadership was stuck in the past and fixated on all the reasons they couldn't engage Millennial talent. As a result, morale was tanking. Negativity and doubt is both detrimental and highly contagious—especially when it comes from the leadership—and *that* is why this organization had an employee engagement problem.

Maybe outside forces were challenging the organization, but it was the attitudes and responses to those challenges that were destroying the organization's ability to keep Millennial talent. If these leaders dedicated even half their energy towards planning for the company's future and involved young talent in the process of creating an organization that is exciting, fulfilling, meaningful, and fun, I am certain their employee engagement problems would disappear.

## Myth: Hire for skills

If turnover is continuous in your organization, and you are certain your team is creating a meaningful and exciting work experience, it's possible you aren't hiring the right people. The most engaging companies tend to be passionate about their missions and they make sure the people they hire to work there feel the same way. In the Industrial Era, skills were enough. In the Talent Economy, screening for culture and job fit takes precedence.

In the late 2000s I toured I Love Rewards, an employee recognition company based in Toronto (the company changed its name to Achievers in 2011). I Love Rewards was way ahead of its time, truly a Talent Economy pioneer, creating an especially unique and collaborative work experience. The company's dedication to job fit was significant.

At the time, I Love Rewards was experiencing a huge growth curve and the CEO, Razor Suleman, didn't want to waste time or resources by hiring the wrong team members. He also wanted to ensure he was hiring the best of the best, which is why he used a four-step interview process:

1. The first step was an open house, which attracted as many as 400 candidates. This introduced prospects to the company and gave the CEO an opportunity to personally meet every candidate.

2. Outstanding candidates were invited to come back for a group interview, usually in groups of 12. Half of the interview time was

spent asking the group questions, and half of the interview was spent asking the prospects to "sell" the company in front of the group.

3. Selected candidates then moved on to a skills interview, for which they were asked to perform a job-related task.

4. During the fourth and final phase of the interviewing process, the prospect provided a comprehensive career history form, describing the prospect's professional journey from high school to the present. The interview itself lasted two to three hours and explored the applicant's education, work experience, and career goals. The leading candidates then arranged phone calls between the CEO and bosses from all the jobs they held in the past 10 years.

Personally, I've made the mistake of hiring fast, and every time it's backfired. Either the skills weren't right or the passion wasn't there, and that mismatch quickly becomes apparent and the employer-employee relationship becomes strained. No matter what the work environment, you simply can't engage someone who doesn't have the skills or the passion that the organization needs.

## Myth: More fun = more engaged

I previously mentioned the importance of creating an organization that is exciting, fulfilling, meaningful, and fun. But I want to be clear that "perks" don't an engaged employee make. Google has won countless awards for being a great place to work, but people started to mistake the physical work environment as the reason for employee engagement.

Indeed, ping pong tables, snacks, beer, and beanbag chairs are fun. But your company doesn't have to have a ping pong table to engage employees. That's like saying you chose your best friend because he has a ping pong table in his basement. The ping pong table might make hanging out at his house fun, but that's not why you consider him your closest friend.

Remember: Perks can potentially serve for attraction, but they aren't going to serve for retention. Employee engagement is the result of a great relationship, and fun is only one part of relationship.

## Myth: Engagement is driven by managers, not the CEO

Engaged employees are committed employees—so absorbed in and enthusiastic about the work that they are willing to further the organization's reputation or interests. In other words, engaged employees are committed to the relationship they have with their employers.

Obviously, leaders are factored into the employer-employee relationship, yet we rarely hear people talk about leadership engagement. Perhaps that's because we just expect leaders to be engaged and committed to the relationship they have with their employees, but data proves otherwise.

In a survey of 500,000 business and HR leaders conducted by Waggl Human Capital Pulse, 97 percent said they believed that listening to employees and incorporating their ideas was critical to an organization's success. However, 38 percent agreed with the statement that hearing from employees once a year through an annual survey gives them the timely insights they need.

Leaders recognize listening to employees is important, but far too many severely limit when and how much they listen. How effective would our relationships be if we limited our contact with the important people in our lives to once a year? Via a survey, no less. Can you imagine sending your relatives or close friends a relationship-survey?

How satisfied are you with our relationship? (Check one)
- ☐ Very
- ☐ Occasionally
- ☐ Somewhat
- ☐ Not at all

Of course, you wouldn't do this. Your employee relationships are different from your personal relationships. Or are they? We're in the Talent Economy. People are driving today's economy, which means we're all in the relationship-building business.

Jackie Safier, mentioned at the beginning of this chapter, spends an incredible amount of time listening to others. This practice not only furthers her relationships with employees and stakeholders, it creates a pipeline of feedback and ideas and ensures her business is successful regardless of what changes or challenges may come Prometheus' way.

Engage with employees on a personal level. Start with an open discussion with employees—of all ages. Let people freely speak their minds, take notes on the feedback they offer, and respond to it. Introduce small-group lunches that have a "no work talk" rule. Or do what the CEO of Namely, an HR and benefits platform, does. He moves his desk every four weeks so he can sit with a new team and build relationships throughout the company.

If there's anything we can learn from the reality show Undercover Boss, it's that leadership is often woefully separated from its workforce and unaware of what they want and need. Each episode of the Emmy award-winning show depicts a person who has an upper-management position at a major business deciding to go undercover as an entry-level employee to discover the faults in the company. And those faults are usually much worse than the boss ever imagined.

Employee engagement isn't rocket science. If your organization is intentional about building relationships with its employees, people will enjoy coming to work. And when people enjoy coming to work, they are more likely to go the extra mile, and they will treat customers better, innovate, and continuously improve the business.

## Time for Change

Employee engagement isn't rocket science, but it could just as well be. Some companies are very successful at adapting to change and building relationships, but with Gallup reporting that nearly 70 percent of the workforce is unengaged, this is not the norm by a long shot. The question isn't whether we should be addressing employee engagement. The question is, "How?" Most organizations fall into one of the following three buckets:

- *The Changemakers:* These are the organizations that give their employees more time to think. Change thrives in these organizations because there tends to be more flexibility, fewer rules, and more trust.

- *The Explosives:* These organizations have more demanding leaders and very specific rules, which create agitation, and sooner or later something blows up. There isn't much time dedicated to thinking about the future or implementing change. These organizations are reactive, not proactive.

- *The Ostriches:* Just as ostriches have a reputation for sticking their heads in the sand, these are the complacent companies which never see change coming. They take comfort in their legacy brands and history of success, insisting "everything is just fine" and "we can ride this out." They tend to be blindsided by change.

Lisa Bodell, CEO of FutureThink, believes that 80 percent of companies fall into the Ostrich category. "All of a sudden, the dimmer switch comes up and these companies go, 'Where did Uber come from? Airbnb, where has that been?' Those signals were there all along. They just didn't want to see them," she said.

The first step toward employee engagement is to identify how your organization approaches change and relationship-building. The Changemakers spend a considerable amount of time thinking about change and preparing for it. They also spend a considerable amount of time on talent generation, thinking about how to hire the best and build the best teams. The other two types of companies are heavily focused on the day-to-day, investing little time or effort into the concepts of talent or change. This makes employee engagement a constant struggle.

Organizations not only need to spend more time thinking about the future and the people who are going to get them there, they need to act. To effectively introduce a change, start by exploring the reason a change is needed with your team of people.

"Everyone always talks about wanting to make a change. But what kind of change? How much change? How much risk are you willing to take?," Bodell noted. Determining why change is needed and where and when will crystallize the team's thinking, making success more likely.

It's also key to pinpoint where employee engagement is happening, and where it's not. Employee engagement is the emotional commitment the employee has with an organization and its goals. This commitment means engaged employees care about their work and the organization. Employee engagement thrives on emotions, experiences, and relationships.

Do you know what inspires your employees or what hurdles prevent them from becoming engaged employees? If not, you should find out.

- *The Organization:* Do employees feel engaged in the organization's mission, culture, and values? Do employees feel engaged in the organization's strategy for success?

- *The Work:* Do employees consider the work that needs to be done as valued and necessary? Do they feel they have access to the knowledge, skills and tools, and connections needed to get the job done?

- *The Team:* Do employees feel the team they are working with can achieve their goals? Do they feel they can trust other employees, give advice to others, or ask others for help?

- *The Network:* Do employees feel engaged with clients, customers, volunteers, and members in professional or social settings outside of work? Do they feel engaged in a network or community via their work?

Engaging people is impossible until you understand them, which can only come from time spent pursuing a relationship with them. When a relationship is non-existent, that's when unconscious bias and distrust creep in.

The chart on the next page helps to highlight some of the key workforce influences and differences by generation. While the chart serves as a helpful, quick reference, it's important to recognize that too much emphasis on the differences themselves can create negative stereotypes and even lead to discrimination.

## Millennial Discrimination

Entitled. Demanding. Lazy. Arrogant. These are just a few of the words used to describe young professionals today. No matter what they achieve or do we place upon them the "mark of immaturity," just as Zuckerberg, the youngest self-made millionaire in history, received on the day of Facebook's IPO.

In Chapter 1, I referred to the Talent Economy, which dawned in 1998 and has since given significant influence to young people. So why, nearly two decades later, are we still struggling to accept and respect them?

History has a lot to do with it.

Anyone who was in the workforce prior to 1998 recalls an era when young people had to pay their dues—given the most mundane tasks, the dirtiest jobs, and the worst shifts. It was believed this would build

# Workforce Differences by Generation

|  | Baby Boomers | Gen X | Gen Y | Gen Z |
|---|---|---|---|---|
| **Born** | 1946–1964 | 1965–1981 | 1982–1995 | 1996–2009 |
| **Size** | 78 million | 48 million | 80 million | 60 million |
| **Nicknames** | Me Generation, The Gray Ceiling | Slackers, MTV Generation | Millennials, Echo Boomers | Centennials, Homelanders |
| **Characteristics** | Hard-working, loyal, confident, competitive | Anti-authority, self-reliant, family focused | Confident, collaborative, needy | Independent, confident, sincere, determined |
| **Why They Are the Way They Are** | Wealthiest generation. Raised to pursue the American Dream. | Latch-key kids, downsizing, cable TV. Raised to be self-sufficient. | Micro-managed by parents. Raised to be high achievers. | Mobile tech. Raised amidst disruption and connectivity. |
| **Communication Styles** | Detailed dialogue in-person or via phone. | Clear, concise communication via e-mail. | Details, frequent feedback, both in-person and online. | Quick, concise via text, photos, or videos. |
| **Problems They Are Facing Now** | Retirement, keeping up with technology. | Debt, work-life balance, career advancement. | Debt, finding the right job, being taken seriously. | Deciphering career path, financial concerns. |
| **What They Want at Work** | Opportunities to lead and leave a legacy. | Opportunities to further their careers. | Opportunities to access new skills, information. | Opportunities to learn, lead, volunteer, create. |
| **Work Styles** | Want to lead. Like to manage others, hold meetings and discuss strategies. | Want autonomy. Hate being micromanaged, wasting time. | Want structure, mentoring, feedback, responsibility. | Want to problem-solve and make a positive difference. |
| **Flaws** | "Been there done that" attitude, not always open to new ideas. | "Wait-and-see" approach, skeptical, difficulty committing. | Ask "what's in it for me?," short attention spans, high demands. | "We can do more/better" approach and high expectations. |
| **Turn-offs** | Questioning their abilities, suggesting something new. | Being overlooked, loyalty that goes unrewarded. | Monitored use of technology, dismissed for lack of experience. | Conformity, dishonesty, lack of creativity. |

character in young people. This "kids-treated-badly-builds-character" methodology dates back to the mid-to-late 1700s, when the Industrial Revolution started to boom and the need for labor increased.

Families migrated from their farms to newly industrialized cities to find work. Unfortunately, factory owners took advantage of the adequate supply of workers. There were plenty of people who were willing to work, and who desperately needed the work, so employers kept wages extremely low and demanded that employees work long hours to keep their jobs.

To survive even the lowest level of poverty, families had to have every member of the family go to work. This included children, and this is where the ill-treatment of youth in the workplace began:

### 1750

In Britain, 14 percent of factory workers were under the age of 14. Children were paid only a fraction of what adults would receive, and were subject to beatings and other harsh forms of pain infliction for being late or not working up to quota. Factory owners loved child labor, arguing it was good for the economy and the building of children's characters. Parents were forced to approve because they needed the income.

### 1833

The Factory Act passed by British Parliament. The act required children to attend school for no less than two hours during the day and also limited the number of hours children could work. (Children 9–13 years-old were limited to 8 hours; 14–18 year olds could only work 12 hours a day). As the Industrial Era expanded into America, these labor practices continued.

Outside of factory work, every skill was something gained almost exclusively by experience. You had to be the apprentice first. There was much to learn from your elders, and it took time to do so. You didn't have anything of credibility to offer, because you didn't have experience. You had to start at the bottom, and you wouldn't move up until someone else allowed you to move up via a promotion. There simply was no other option.

Although our society has become more educated and our economy has diversified, there are still remnants of the Industrial Era everywhere—not excluding how we treat young professionals. Some organizations still put a high value on experience, quick to criticize or ignore the contributions of young people.

Age discrimination is often thought of as a problem for older workers, but lately, there are signs that persistent myths and stereotypes about Millennials are dampening the appetite for hiring younger people, with some companies reporting they are reluctant to hire anyone under the age of 40.

It's become common for older workers to label young professionals as somehow different or difficult. You've heard the criticism; people who complain "young professionals these days" are simply entitled trophy kids who suffer from Peter Pan-syndrome, returning home to live in their parent's basements, unwilling to accept the responsibility of adulthood, and unable to cope with pressure or adversity. Or the people who say young people are pushing older generations out and should just get in line and wait their turns.

To that second point, I'm not advocating for anyone to be pushed out of the way. I'm advocating for the opportunity to work together. It's not about competition. It's about collaboration. To the first point, it can easily be argued that Millennials have faced considerable challenges and disparagement as older generations have continued to ostracize them or avoid hiring them. These fears tend to be based on myths and stereotypes, forcing us to look for the negative rather than the positive in every generation. This makes collaboration, productivity, and employee engagement a nearly impossible feat.

Until we can truly understand and empathize with one another, we can't move forward. What's the reality behind each of these Millennial stereotypes?

## Myth: They're lazy

The Millennial generation has a reputation for being lazy, retreating home to live with mom and dad, and unwilling to do whatever it takes to make ends meet, despite the fact they've had access to more education, technology, and job opportunities than any other generation.

The Millennial generation is the best-educated generation in history, with 34 percent having at least a bachelor's degree. But they are also the first generation in modern history to have high levels of student loan debt, poverty, and unemployment combined with low levels of wealth and personal income. The fact is, the transition to careers and financial independence has been largely riddled with roadblocks for this generation. Consider these economic truths:

- *For starters, it's become increasingly difficult to make it on a high school diploma alone.*

  Historically, Americans who didn't attend college (or even complete high school) had an abundant job market available to them. Working as farmers or factory workers, unskilled workers made less but they were still able to make a decent living and even secure a middle-class lifestyle for their families. In 1979, a high school graduate earned 77 percent of what a college graduate earned; today, a high school diploma will get you 62 percent of what a college graduate earns. This disparity in economic outcomes has never been greater.

- *Seeing no other option, many Millennials pursued higher education despite rising tuition costs.*

College tuition has observed a 1,140 percent increase since the late 1970s, coupled with the longest stretch of income stagnation in the modern era. Pew Research reports that the average college debt for a Millennial is $33,000. Student loan debt in the United States has reached $1.3 trillion dollars—more than credit card and auto loan debt combined.

- *The economy crashed when many Millennials were enrolled in college.*
  Millennials were entering the workforce during the nation's deepest recession in decades. A growing number are working in low-wage industries and earning less than their predecessors. For example, in 2016, the New York City Comptroller's Office released a report stating that young workers in America's largest city are earning about 20 percent less than the generation before them did at the same age, even after adjusting for inflation and changes to the cost of living.

- *The recession delayed retirements, making it difficult for Millennials to find jobs.*
  While the job market has continued to recover, Millennials have increasingly been left out. For example, between September 2015 and February 2016, the U.S. economy added a little over 2 million jobs. Yet, the number of workers aged 20 to 24 declined by just over 200,000 jobs during that same period, while employment among workers aged 55 and over increased by 742,000.

- *The jobs that are readily available simply don't pay enough.*
  In many cases, wages have remained stagnant. Economists say this lack of wage growth proves the United States has a demand problem (not enough good jobs), rather than a supply problem (not enough skilled workers). Millennials have come of age during the worst recession and the longest stretch of income stagnation in the modern era. While salary isn't everything to this

generation, it still matters as they have continually struggled to make ends meet.

All these reasons explain why we're seeing baristas working at Starbucks who have Master's degrees, and why the highest percentage of 20-somethings ever recorded (around 35 percent) are back living with their parents. It's also why an estimated 40 percent of unemployed workers are Millennials, 88 percent of minimum-wage workers are age 20 or older, and 4 in 10 minimum wage workers are college graduates. It's not a matter of being lazy. This generation is working hard to simply establish their careers and financial independence.

## Myth: They're entitled

When Xers and Boomers were children, they would leave the house in the morning and disappear for hours, off exploring and playing. Parents didn't really track their children's whereabouts. As long as children were home in time for dinner, all was well. That certainly wasn't the case with Millennials.

Millennials are the most protected, supervised, provided for generation in history. Raised by the wealthiest generation in history—the Baby Boomers—most Millennials had very structured childhoods. They never ventured far from home or spent much time on their own and were frequently shuttled around to soccer practices and playdates in car seats and bike helmets, under the constant guidance of their helicopter parents. From the time they were young, they were raised as mini-adults, given time-outs instead of discipline, encouraged to talk about their feelings, asked to share their opinions, and influenced household purchasing decisions.

It's not hard to understand why other generations would assume this generation is more self-absorbed, whiny, and spoiled, considering they were rarely left to figure things out for themselves or use their imaginations, and spent most of their childhood in a close relationship with their parents, teachers, and coaches.

It's also not hard to understand why Millennials would hate the Millennial label, seeking to distance themselves from an identity that has often been equated with being entitled, difficult, or immature.

In any case, these negative stereotypes are doing considerable damage, discouraging collaboration, productivity, employee engagement, and communication.

Adam and Alison are Millennials who are afraid to speak up at work, because they feel like their older colleagues stereotype and criticize them simply for being Millennials. (I've omitted their last names to protect their privacy.)

### Adam

Adam knows he should be feeling excited about his first job, but the opportunity has been greatly overshadowed by his feeling of loneliness. In fact, he describes the feeling he gets at work as "the loneliest I've ever felt in my entire life."

Adam grew up participating in organized sports, attending daycare and after school programs, collaborating on team projects at school, living with roommates in college, and moving in with six roommates after college because he couldn't afford to buy his own apartment.

On the first day of his new job, his manager showed Adam to his new office, then walked out. Adam said he just stood there, panicked, and unsure of what to do. "The boss just said to me, 'There's your office, now go do your job.' But I've never, ever done anything by myself! I'm used to working with people, not for people. I had no idea what to do."

Adam is miserable, but he's afraid to tell anyone how he really feels. "My co-workers are older and very critical of people in my generation. I know they will think I'm just another entitled Millennial who can't think for himself and needs constant attention."

### Alison

Alison is angry at her colleagues. Like Adam, she's one of the youngest people on staff, and her co-workers have openly criticized her for being a Millennial.

"They assume that I'm entitled and expect to receive trophies," she said. "What I really want to say to them is, 'We were children! Our parents and teachers and coaches were the ones who decided to give us trophies. We certainly didn't hand out trophies to ourselves!' And now everyone criticizes us for something we didn't do and had no control over. Those same adults who gave us trophies are now blaming us for being entitled. I just don't understand it."

Ageism is alive and well in our society. It's the last bastion of workforce discrimination. We're so aware of diversity and inclusion now, and most of us wouldn't openly discriminate by race, gender, sexual preference, or religion, yet it's somehow acceptable to make disrespectful comments about other generations.

In 2013, Stephen Parkhurst, a New York filmmaker, turned the tables. He'd had enough of hearing how his generation was lazy, so he created a controversial mini-film titled, *Millennials: We Suck and We're Sorry.* He got the idea for the project after reading articles critical of Millennials, specifically referring to them as entitled and lazy. The three-minute film features actors in their 20s and dishes out some harsh, sarcastic commentary directed towards the Boomer generation.

One section from the film states:

"It's not like we jacked-up college tuition prices or destroyed the manufacturing industry, started two quagmire wars, gutted the unions, destroyed the global economy, and left our offspring with an environmentally devastated planet stripped of its natural resources. It would be crazy if there was a generation that recklessly awful."

Ouch! And the generation-on-generation hate isn't limited to Boomers and Millennials.

Recently, I received a call from a prospective client. I'd never met this person before, but I knew he was a well-respected and accomplished leader in his industry. During the conversation, he told me how much he loved my books and admired the work I was doing, and I felt flattered. Then to my shock, he added, "Thank goodness you're not a Gen Xer! I would never work with an Xer. I avoid them whenever possible. They are an entire generation of complainers and slackers. At least the Millennials were raised by Boomers and have some work ethic." I ended the call shortly after that comment, partly because I don't want to work with someone who makes blatant attacks on others—but mostly because I'm a Gen Xer.

We all desire to be relevant and important. But tearing down others to make ourselves feel more relevant and important is not just ignorant and discriminative, but also likely another reason we're losing $30.5 billion in employee turnover each year.

Yes, Millennials are the first generation to be rewarded for participation, and they were raised by the wealthiest generation in history. But that's not to say they haven't experienced hardships. Millennials were raised during a recession, amidst widespread outbreaks of terrorism and school shootings.

Seeking to understand what has influenced this generation, to listen and collaborate, to empathize rather than stereotype or criticize, are the trademarks of both a great leader and a great place to work.

## Myth: They're quitters

Another fear employers have is that young workers simply won't stick with a job once hired—that some other opportunity will catch their eye and they'll be off, leaving the employer high and dry. Indeed, the Millennial generation is notorious for job-hopping. According to Gallup, more than 20 percent of Millennials have changed jobs in the past year, which is three times more frequent than older adults. In Deloitte's survey of 7,000 Millennials, more than 40 percent plan to leave their jobs within the next 24 months.

But rather than chalk this up to being a character flaw, we should be asking why. Why are Millennials more likely to leave? What's causing these high rates of employee turnover and what can employers do to reduce it?

In 2016, XYZ University surveyed 502 Millennials from 45 states and authored a research paper on the turnover epidemic. The conclusion: This is a changed generation, uniquely influenced by recession, competition, education, technology, and so much more. They take their career choices very seriously, and turnover will likely continue to be prevalent until Millennials find what they seek, which has been influenced primarily by their financial, emotional, and educational needs.

Here are the ten reasons Millennials cited for quitting their jobs:

### 1. They want to take risks.

Trying to enter the workforce during a recession meant Millennials had to endure high unemployment and salary cuts, and many were forced to take lower-paying jobs because that's what was available to them. Many experts predicted the recession would make people feel grateful to have a job, but it had quite the opposite effect on Millennials; the experience encouraged them to take more risks.

Nadira Hira, author of the forthcoming book, *Misled: How a Generation of Leaders Lost the Faith (And Just What You'll Need to Get It Back)*, notes how graduating into the recession has changed her generation's attitude toward work in general. "It's made us recognize how short life actually is. We don't want to be like our parents have been, investing 30 years in a company only to be unceremoniously laid-off at the end of it all," she said.

"Maybe it's counter-intuitive, but the recession made me and a lot of other people much braver about our decision-making. In past generations, you just put your head down and hoped for the best. This generation—myself included—learned that you can't put your head down and hope for the best, because that's not a successful strategy."

### 2. They're investing into education.

Prior generations were likely to enter the workforce shortly after high school or college, working full-time by their early 20s. That's not the case with Millennials. Millennials are the most educated generation to date, spending more time and money on education. Nearly 60 percent juggle jobs and education at the same time.

The investment into education has led to delays in other adult transitions. Millennials are waiting longer than any other generation to marry and have children, whereas in the past having a family that depended on your income was one reason to stay in a job. With marriage and parenthood moving down their list of priorities, this generation has had the independence and flexibility to explore career opportunities.

### 3. They want a job that fits their identity.

When it comes to jobs, Millennials have considerably more choices than previous generations. This is due to the massive retirement wave currently underway, alongside the creation of entirely new industries (like cyber security), and start-ups that didn't exist just 10 years ago. With so many career options and fewer obligations to family, Millennials have the time and opportunity to be selective about job fit.

Unlike previous generations, Millennials don't just think of work as something they *do*; they see it as central part of who they *are*. In the Clark University Poll of Emerging Adults, 79 percent of 18- to 29-year-olds felt it's more important to enjoy their job than it is to have a high salary.

Millennials are looking for the ideal, which is a job that really inspires them and helps to define their values. "So if they have a job they're not that crazy about—even if it makes decent money and has good benefits—they might quit because they find something they think is closer to the ideal," explained Dr. Jeffrey Jensen Arnett, a research psychologist at Clark University.

### 4. They want to stay competitive.

Millennials recognize that a rapidly shifting job market means they need to constantly be improving to stay competitive. "Millennials want their employers to help them grow their skills—not just help them pay their bills," stated Aimee Schuster, Vice President of Marketing at Yello, a talent acquisition software company.

The 2016 Yello Recruiting Study, a survey of 7,000 college students and recent graduates, revealed that learning opportunities are key in Millennials' decisions to accept a job. In fact, 48 percent of respondents cited learning opportunities as the most important factor when accepting a job offer.

Millennial author and journalist Nadira Hira echoed these sentiments. "In my first job, it wasn't that it was a huge organization that could send me around the world. It was organic. So the photo editor needed help on something; I would go look through all the stock photos with her and pick things. Our graphics editor needed help on something; I'd go sit next to him and design sidebars together. I did everything from pore over expenses with our accountant to answer our editor-in-chief's phone; everyone he spoke to, I spoke to first. And I think the breadth of that experience made me feel like I was getting the full picture, and contributing in so many meaningful ways. That's the kind of learning we all want— being in the trenches, and doing the work alongside the people who do it best."

She added, "The places where I've been most happy, it's because I've been allowed to take initiative and push boundaries, to apply my natural entrepreneurial spirit to what the organization does and advance our mission together."

### 5. They want to make a difference.

Millennials have been raised in an era of incredible change. They watched technology change the way people lived, worked, and did business, and terrorism and the recession both left lasting impressions on this generation. These changes—both positive and negative—instilled in them high hopes for moving into jobs where they, too, can make changes and a meaningful difference.

In the Clark University Poll of Emerging Adults, 86 percent of 18-to-29 year-olds felt it was important to have a career that does some good in the world. When Millennials do not see a deeper meaning to their work, they are likely to disengage and leave, explained Brett Farmiloe, a Millennial and founder of Markitors, a digital marketing company.

In 2007, Farmiloe and four other new college grads were corporately sponsored to travel across America to find out what makes people passionate about their work. The tour was inspired by the stat that half of the American workforce is unhappy with their jobs. Farmiloe and team visited 38 states and conducted 300 interviews. He said the culture and the purpose within most companies simply aren't compelling enough to keep Millennials engaged.

### 6. They want to be mentored.

Pew Research reported in 2016 that for the first time in more than 130 years, adults ages 18 to 34 are more likely to be living with a parent than living with a spouse or on their own. Millennials have been raised in close connectivity with the adults in their lives, which is why they see their managers and supervisors as playing a crucial role in helping them develop as employees.

Millennials feel loyal to the people who have advocated for them, who have treated them well, and who have helped them grow. Derrick Duplessy is a Millennial and the executive director of the Duplessy Foundation and host of Purpose Rockstar Podcast. He said Millennials will ask themselves: Do I have the tools, the plans, the step-by-step that's necessary for me to be successful?

"Millennials want to feel like, 'Wow! Someone is really investing in me, and paying attention to me!' Because often, we feel like we're given the work, and we're asked to do the work, but beyond that nobody really cares about us as a person or as a professional," he said. "Just being intentional about mentoring and training young employees goes a long way toward keeping them around."

### 7. They want to use their skills.

"I don't want to fix a copy machine, I want to be able to manage a membership program, and do all those things that are actually professionally fulfilling," stated Ashley Sullivan, deputy executive director at GWA: The Association for Garden Communicators.

For many employers, the instinctive response to high turnover is to invest less in new employees. Why sink lots of time and effort into training new hires if they are just going to turn around and leave in a few months? Considering that many in this generation view jobs as résumé-builders rather than final destinations, investing in Millennials' skills can feel ineffective or even dangerous.

However, research clearly indicates Millennials value opportunities to learn and grow. Their job satisfaction is reliant on their ability to learn, which means employers risk losing Millennials when they do train them, and also when they don't.

### 8. They want the truth.

Sullivan said feeling misled was a major factor in her decision to leave a former employer. "I kept finding myself saying, 'This isn't what I really signed up for or what I thought I was signing up for.'"

While every business has tedious and repetitive tasks that need to be done, making the reasons clear to employees will contribute to their sense of purpose. "If I'm doing something repetitive I need to know what it's leading to. That's the motivating factor. If the end result is meaningful, then people will go through the tedium," Duplessy explained.

Farmiloe agrees that honesty is the best policy, and extremely important to Millennials. "If a job is going to be difficult, stressful, or boring, acknowledge that during recruitment," he advised. He added that painting a very unrealistic picture of the job not only leads to disillusionment, negativity, and turnover, it could also "discourage the kind of people that you really wanted from applying in the first place."

### 9. They want flexibility.

More than past generations, Millennials have come to expect some flexibility in their work schedules. Technology has made it easier than ever to work anywhere, and Millennials know there are many tasks they can perform just as easily from home as they can at the office. This has led many Millennials to question the traditional norms that dictate work schedules.

When companies do afford Millennials some freedom in their work schedules, it is often noticed and appreciated. Sullivan said it is "comforting" to Millennials to know they are working for an employer who is sympathetic and understanding, and trusts the employees to use their time wisely.

### 10. They got a better offer.

Thirty-five percent of XYZ University survey-takers and 27 percent of Yello Recruiting Study survey takers said they left their previous job because they were given a better opportunity elsewhere. Given their financial concerns, desire for flexibility and honesty, and search for purpose and job fit, it makes sense that Millennials would be willing to job-hop if a better offer presented itself.

Turnover is an indication that Millennials haven't found what they need. The more employers understand the reasons for turnover—and create an environment that is inclusive to Millennials—the more likely it is that employers will be capable of retaining their talent. If Millennials can find the jobs they seek, the turnover is likely to decrease. Until then, employee turnover among this generation is likely to continue, and even worsen, amidst the pending skills shortage and talent war.

Does this mean Millennials are lazy, entitled, or quitters? No. It means the work environment your organization is providing doesn't make sense to this generation or isn't inviting to them. And the reason it doesn't make sense to them is because society has evolved—before most Millennials were even in the workplace.

In 1998, when the Talent Economy arrived, the oldest Millennials were 16. Google wasn't founded by two Millennials; it was founded by Gen Xers. The Talent Economy emerged under the watch of the Boomers and Gen Xers, yet they are the ones struggling the most to adapt.

It's like blaming Millennials for being "Trophy Kids," when it was the adults who gave them the trophies in the first place. It makes no sense to blame the Millennials for expecting their employers to be evolved and utilizing 21st-century management practices, when the evolution to a talent-centric economy started before most of them even had their first jobs.

Millennials came of age in this era of disruption, and they are the outcome of this era of disruption. But even before they were in the workforce, everything about the way we live, work, and do business was changing (or should have been) to keep up with advancements spurred by technology, education, and innovation. All this change and disruption is presenting more opportunities than ever before, yet employers are holding steadfast to the traditions of the past, struggling to respect and accept younger generations, much less work together.

Until we can recognize and implement collaboration as the best strategy to successfully navigate the future, we'll remain fearfully stuck on a hamster wheel, running in place, repeatedly reminded that our leadership is aging, our leadership practices are failing, and employee engagement is declining.

## Trust

Engaging people is impossible until you understand them, which can only come from time spent pursuing a relationship with them. Once you move into that phase, it's more probable the organization can achieve employee engagement, which really comes down to trust.

Great Place to Work has been studying and recognizing great places to work for 30 years, likely best known for producing the annual *Fortune* 100 Best Companies to Work For® list as well as over a dozen other Best Workplaces lists in partnership with *Fortune.*

Contrary to popular belief, great places to work aren't built on perks or benefits. Jessica Rohman, Director of Content at Great Place to Work said all the buzz around on-site massages, extended paternity leave, paid sabbaticals, and bring-your-dog-to-work-day catches media attention because it's fun and interesting. "But the actual component of great workplaces is trust. In our 30 years of research at Great Place to Work, trust is the element time and time again that sets the best companies apart from the rest," she said.

Rohman said the best places to work demonstrate trust in three ways:

1. Employees believe their leaders are credible. The leaders' actions match their words, they are transparent with their communication, and they are competent at doing their jobs.

2. Employees believe their leaders respect them, both as professionals and as people who have lives outside of work.

3. Employees believe their leaders are fair. The leaders create a level playing field where all employees are treated fairly and given equal access to opportunities and recognition, regardless of race, gender, or other personal characteristics.

"Being a great place to work is rooted in trust and trust is built by leaders. They set the tone for how people relate to each other, what information can be shared, how information is shared, how employees are developed and treated. They even set the tone for what the purpose of the organization is and why the organization exists, and how people are connected to that purpose across the organization," Rohman said.

This aligns with what Nicole Martin said about the 101 Best and Brightest; the CEOs care about their employees and this is evident in their actions and furthers trust.

When Great Place to Work started its research of successful companies in 1981, the concept of organizational culture was considered a "touchy, feely thing" with no business benefit, Rohman said. Since then, research and metrics have proven that great places to work are more engaging, have less turnover, and therefore higher productivity and healthier bottom lines.

As a result, the external pressure for leaders to be future-focused and dedicated to relationship-building has increased, and will continue to do so. The new workforce has little patience for the ideals of an Industrial-Era organization; CEOs will be forced to decide whether they want to keep the best talent and those that do will remain competitive.

Unlike other generations, Millennials have been raised in this era that celebrates and understands great workplace cultures. "Millennials are known for job-hopping. It's not that they're inherently disloyal or something like that, it's that the Millennial generation has the expectation of a great workplace," Rohman said.

These expectations exist because Millennials have been raised knowing that healthy, happy workplaces exist, and learning that work-life balance is an important life value. Therefore, Millennials won't settle for less. They expect to have trust-based relationships with their managers, a sense of purpose and pride in their work, and the sense of being connected to other people and to something that's bigger than themselves.

"It goes far beyond pay. Obviously, companies need to pay their employees fairly, but there's a lot more that goes into creating that fulfilling sense of a workplace. Millennials have really tapped into this and are, quite frankly, demanding it through their actions. They're showing if their employers don't have those things, they will leave," she said.

Whereas a great culture used to be a "nice to have," now business leaders around the world are shifting their focus to culture as a strategic business priority. Research shows the voluntary turnover at companies that are named Great Places to Work is about half as much in comparison to industry peers, and the number of people who believe they're being paid fairly is far higher among the great workplaces than others. Specifically, Millennials are 25 times more likely to say they want to stay at a Great Place to Work employer for a long time.

Trust isn't making headlines, but it is the precursor to employee engagement. "You won't be engaged if you don't trust. To engage with other people, that takes vulnerability, and trust underlies vulnerability. So first comes trust," Rohman said.

The employees working at a Great Place to Work know that their employers have their best interests at heart, care about them, and are trustworthy. "It's all the things that you have in every healthy relationship in your life," Rohman said.

## Building Bridges

Michelle Grocholsky, Director of Inclusion and Engagement for RICS (Royal Institute of Chartered Surveyors), explained how the historic organization embarked on a change initiative. RICS was founded in London in 1868, receiving a Royal charter in 1881.

"Our organization was at a crossroads. We've been in existence since the 1800s, so as you can imagine, our organization was still very traditional, revered, and historic. We realized the need for evolution," Grocholsky explained.

For starters, RICS had to start challenging assumptions. "We recognized the opportunity to think differently about our talent mix. Specifically, the diversity of skills, experiences, and capabilities that will enable us to innovate and understand and meet the needs of our diverse marketplace," Grocholsky said.

With the lion share of development work in the land, property, and construction sector emerging within countries like India, Africa, and China, RICS knew that their business and talent plan needed to shift to these countries as well. Work was done to identify how business practices and the RICS culture could adapt to attract high-caliber and multi-generational talent across regions, to help the organization grow its market presence and reputation as a leading professional body within the sector.

"We started having conversations externally, with the industry, to try to shift our thinking towards the future, how to anticipate change, and move into a different direction," Grocholsky said. At the same time, RICS looked inward, realizing the team needed to further its relationships, establish trust, and successfully adapt to a changing workforce.

To aid in this effort, RICS launched Dare to Share. Employees are encouraged to record two- to four-minute videos on their smart phones in which they share something personal about themselves. For example, employees have shared videos explaining what it's like to live and work with a disability, or explaining their battle to overcome social anxiety. Videos were posted on a private communication platform for the RICS team and proved hugely beneficial in forming connections between colleagues from across the world.

RICS also introduced inclusion coaching for every member of the executive team, and began having team dialogues about employee empowerment. "We had too much bureaucracy and this was a real barrier for our employees who felt they couldn't make any decisions," Grocholsky said. Employees were asked to help develop programs to remove these barriers, empower employees, and rebuild the team.

In the Industrial Era, how senior management was treated and felt mattered the most. Everyone else was expected to just do their jobs and find satisfaction and fulfillment in a paycheck. In the Talent Economy, relationships with employees matter most—all employees. In fact, as we move further into the Talent Economy, it's become increasingly apparent that being in a relationship with an organization's newest, youngest employees is critical to creating future-focused, relevant organizations, navigating disruption, and maintaining employee engagement.

CEOs are now standing at a critical crossroads and must choose to focus on talent generation if they want their organizations to compete, or even survive. It's imperative we learn from the success stories of firms like Prometheus Real Estate Group who have not only been able to engage employees throughout an era of decline and disruption, they have emerged as leaders, boasting incredible success.

Jackie Safier made a commitment to excellence and being a revolutionary when she was named CEO. She has kept Prometheus on the cutting edge by continually seeking the insights of others. In a recent awards acceptance speech she said, "The credit for this award goes to our Prometheans (employees); they have built the culture here in every way."

But the relationships and culture that exist within Prometheus are perhaps best summed up not in Safier's words, but in the words of some of the employees, like these posted on Glassdoor.com:

- "Prometheus is a company unlike any other. The culture, the people, and the revolutionary way things are done in our company is what makes Prometheus the perfect place to call HOME for your career. I couldn't be more proud to work for Prometheus."

- "The culture that this company brings to the table is amazing! You are encouraged to be yourself and have fun. There is always someone there to help you if you have any questions or just need some information. It is a great feeling to know that you get recognized for your hard work and are appreciated!"

- "It has been a privilege and an honor to be a part of the Prometheus brand. I have felt incomparable love and warmth from the Prometheus family, and I have a thorough appreciation for each team member! I'm deeply grateful for the opportunity afforded to me by this outstanding organization! Prometheus is a world-class organization with impeccable standards reinforced by a familial atmosphere that has truly made me feel "at home." I shall remain forever grateful for the support, guidance, and friendship that the Prometheus family extended to me."

It is possible for an Industrial-Era company to succeed in the Talent Economy. That success starts with relationships.

## CHAPTER SUMMARY

According to Gallup, the number of actively engaged employees in the United States has averaged less than 33 percent over the past decade. There are several myths and misunderstandings as to what drives employee engagement and how to achieve it. In addition, there are several myths and misunderstandings of Millennials, leading to discrimination and challenges engaging them.

Engaging people is impossible until you understand them, which can only come from time spent pursuing a relationship with them. Once you practice acceptance and collaboration, it's more probable the organization can achieve employee engagement, which is based on trust.

## QUESTIONS TO CONSIDER

1. This chapter mentions three types of organizations: Changemakers, Explosives, and Ostriches. Which category does your organization fall into? Why?

2. On a scale of 1–5 (1 being awful and 5 being awesome) how would you rank your organization's current proficiency at the following?

    _____ Employees believe their leaders are credible. The leaders' actions match their words, they are transparent with their communication, and they are competent at doing their jobs.

    _____ Employees believe their leaders respect them, both as professionals and as people who have lives outside of work.

    _____ Employees believe their leaders are fair. The leaders create a level playing field where all employees are treated fairly and given equal access to opportunities and recognition, regardless of race, gender, or other personal characteristics.

3. Would you describe yourself as an engaged employee? Why or why not?

4. What could you do to be more accepting of your co-workers, members, or volunteers?

5. What would happen if your organization spent more time and resources focused on collaborating with, building relationships with, or helping advance the careers of young professionals?

*The Talent Generation model relies on two key components: putting people first and maintaining a future focus. To put people first is to value your people more than your profits.*

Build the Future
Education and Business Align

Leadership
Passion, Optimism, Humility, Urgency

Collaborate
Innovation via Team-Building

Acceptance
Inclusion and Trust

Future Focus
Research, Trends, Opportunities

People First
Mission, Vision, and Strategy

*"Don't try to make $1 million.*
*Focus on helping 1 million people."*

DALE PARTRIDGE

CHAPTER 4

...............................

# People First

In 2015, Dan Price, the then 30-year-old CEO of Gravity Payments, surprised his staff with a pay raise. The minimum wage range at the Seattle credit card processing company was bumped up from the average $48,000 salary to $70,000. A video clip from the day of the announcement shows Price telling his 120 employees that he would be taking a pay cut, compensated the same as his employees:

> My pay is based on market rates and what it would cost to replace me. And because of this growing inequality as a CEO, that number is really, really high. My compensation is really high. So I'm actually taking my salary down to the minimum salary as well, until our profit goes up to where it was before we made this policy change.

Price's speech was followed by a standing ovation and whoops of joy from his team. The move prompted considerable controversy, which played out in a firestorm of national media.

Some heralded the switch for more equitable salaries, considering Price was earning $1.1 million. Senator Bernie Sanders said on MSNBC he hoped other CEOs would follow Price's example. Others predicted productivity would plummet along with employees' willingness to strive for the next level. Some media reports stated the wage hike was nothing but a PR stunt and the company was on the verge of collapse. Others went so far as to refer to Price as a psycho-maniac who was living in a fairytale.

Six months into the new pay structure, a Harvard Business School professor analyzed Price's decision, writing about why Price had become the victim of backlash:

> Perhaps Price should have assumed there would be pushback, and consulted with staff and customers about their concerns before implementing it. He might have taken this step more quietly, without such a fanfare. … For now, his story should remind us all that good intentions aren't enough.

Some customers left, worried that the added costs would be passed on to them. Some employees left, frustrated that employees with less skills or ambition would be making the same as them. And heads of other tech companies were "complaining that he has made them look bad by comparison," the Harvard professor reported.

A year after Price's announcement, the media coverage continued, some of it becoming tabloid material, as a few media outlets attacked Price's personal life and mental stability, insinuating that the CEO must have something to hide.

Price's decision set the business world reeling with doubts—to the point of looking for an excuse to dislike, discredit, or distrust his decision. Much like Mark Zuckerberg's story in Chapter 2, the critics preyed upon Price's "mark of immaturity" and discounted him as someone who was too young and inexperienced to know any better.

But 18 months later, it was becoming difficult, if not impossible, to deny Gravity Payments' positive momentum. Since the initial pay hike, considerable changes had occurred within the company and its workforce:

- Employee retention hit an all-time high;
- Employee happiness rates increased;
- Sales nearly doubled, going from $3.5 million to $6.5 million in a single year;
- More than 30,000 job applications had come in, and Gravity had hired 50 new employees;
- The team increased their 401k contributions by 130 percent; and
- Several employees relocated, saving employees an estimated 1,560 hours in annual commute time.

Price has stated that he wants businesses to stop thinking that making money is the most important goal, and to start thinking about purpose, service, and solving the problems of humanity. He wants businesses to realize that when employees are not making enough money to have their basic financial needs met, anxieties become a distraction, and this prohibits their full engagement at work. He argues—and has now proven—that reducing the distraction of money increases engagement and leads to positive business results.

Price has inspired other leaders to follow in his footsteps. Pharmalogics CEO Megan Driscoll saw Price keynote the Inc. 5000 conference in October 2015. By January 2016, she had raised the base salary for all her employees from $38,500 to $50,000. Within a year of the pay increase, Phamalogics' retention grew from 40 percent to 84 percent and the company's workforce grew from 48 employees to 72 with projections to add another 30 employees within the coming year. Price is a pioneer of the Talent Economy, and like other pioneers he's had to endure extreme challenges simply for the sake of blazing a new trail.

## Talent Focus

In the Industrial Era, there was an intense focus on building and scaling. Businesses were built on the backs of workers (literally) and the measurements of success were productivity and profitability. Businesses were fueled by hard work and a concentrated focus on the bottom line.

In the Talent Economy, businesses are being built on brains, not brawn, and the measurement of success is employee engagement—getting employees to care about the organization and the work they do. In the Talent Economy, organizations are fueled by emotion and relationships.

I first met Holly Paul when we both presented at a recruiter conference in New York City. At the time, she was working as the U.S. Talent Acquisition Leader for PwC, managing a team of 300 professionals to hire 11,000 staff annually. Presently, she's the Chief Human Resources Officer for FTI Consulting, overseeing all areas of human capital for employees based in 26 countries.

When I think about wooing talent, I think about Holly Paul. She is very clear about what makes some companies better at engaging employees than others. It's a talent focus. It's valuing your people above everything else, not just in a matter of speaking, but a matter of doing.

Paul referred to PwC as a "talent forward organization." In contrast, when she arrived at FTI, the organization was in the process of developing a talent focus, something the prior CEO didn't have and the new CEO wanted to implement.

Gleaning insights from both work experiences, Paul identified the cornerstones of a talent-focused organization as follows:

- The CEO empowers and encourages employees to unleash their potential.

- There's a laser-focus on talent and the development of talent metrics. "A talent-focused organization discusses employee turnover, engagement, and culture as much as revenue," Paul said.

- Employees are always part of the discussion and their views are included in the strategic plan, which is "not just a business strategy but a human strategy," she said.

- There's an effort to incorporate young talent into everything. Paul referred to this as a "de-layering" effort. "It takes work to get your workforce to think differently about work," she explained. "But we have to bring in young talent and enforce ways to do that throughout the entire organization. Young professionals are key to our future. Without their talent and ideas, an organization will grow stagnant."

Paul noted that the diversity of thought and age has been proven time and again to lead to significant positive bottom-line results, yet she's concerned that far too few organizations are willing to do what it takes to be truly talent-focused.

## People Over Profits

Being truly talent-focused means prioritizing your people above all else—even money. As is evident in Price's case, this practice is still considered a risk by Industrial-Era leaders. Price removed the distraction of money to put the focus on his talent. The client sales followed. Happier employees resulted in happier clients and a better business overall. In the past, talent was the last investment. In today's talent-driven economy, it must be the first. However, we have a long way to go.

In 1965, executive pay in the United States was 24 times worker pay. Now it is a whopping 275 times. In the United Kingdom, CEOs are paid 129 times more than the people who work for them. Sixty percent of UK employees surveyed by the Chartered Institute of Personnel and Development claimed that CEO pay affects their motivation.

Price hit a nerve by offering to cut his own salary to boost the salaries of his employees. Pay disparity had become an accepted barrier to employee engagement, but research overwhelmingly indicates this era of disparity and intense profit-focus is nearing an end.

Glassdoor mined data from more than 615,000 Glassdoor users, grouped by income, who were asked to rank the following as it relates to their job satisfaction:

- Career opportunities
- Compensation and benefits
- Culture and values
- Senior leadership
- Work-life balance
- Business outlook

The most important factor for job satisfaction in Glassdoor's research was the company's culture and values; compensation and benefits came in last. Likewise, Stanford Graduate School research revealed that a meaningful impact on the world is a better predictor of happiness than anything else—even money.

Surprisingly, Glassdoor's research also discovered that interest in how well the company is doing declines as salary increases. The dip could indicate that senior leaders become apathetic, and a little too comfortable with each standard pay raise, losing site of the greater mission and passion for their jobs.

The fact that higher paid workers are less interested in the company's well-being is a red flag. It's important to be aware of your organization's pay structures and to question whether it's negatively affecting employee engagement, morale, or motivation.

Buffer, a social media management platform, shocked the world when it published its Open Salaries Formula, revealing the entire team's salaries as well as the formula used to calculate their salaries. Why would the organization do this? Because one of the highest values Buffer has is transparency. "Transparency breeds trust, and that's one of the key reasons for us to place such a high importance on it. Open salaries are a step towards the ultimate goal of Buffer being a completely Open Company," states the company's website. In addition, the company wants to build "one of the most unique and fulfilling workplaces that exist," and that requires rethinking a lot of traditional practices.

The entire team worked on the development of the salary formula, along with a web app that anyone can use to find out what they would make if they were part of the team at Buffer. The formula is as follows: Role (overall base + location base + cost of living) × Role Value.

The role component consists of the following four factors:

- **Overall Base:** Buffer uses standard U.S. data from both Payscale and Glassdoor to determine 35 percent of the base.

- **Location Base:** Buffer employs staff based in locations all over the world, so for the remaining 65 percent of the base, Buffer factors in each location's cost of living using Numbeo together with data from Payscale and Glassdoor.

- **Cost of Living Correction:** A $0–$8,000 addition to some salaries is added based on a location's market rates. Buffer refers to this as the Good Life Curve. For example, San Francisco and London have a similar cost of living, but very different job markets.

- **Role Value:** Buffer doesn't always agree with the market salary data, so they create their own "role value adjustment" based on what they feel is fair.

- **Experience:** After Buffer has your base salary determined, the experience multiplier is applied, determined through discussions with each team member: Beginner is 1x, Intermediate is 1.1x, Advanced is 1.2x, and Master is 1.3x.

- **Loyalty:** Each year a teammate works at Buffer, the employee receives a general pay raise of 5 percent. This is applied on top of all the above.

- **Choice:** Buffer team members have the option to either receive extra salary (an extra $10,000) or extra stock options (30 percent more) in their compensation packages.

Using this formula, Buffer can easily create a customized compensation package for an advanced engineer, living in Cape Town, who chooses more equity, and has two children and a husband depending on her income.

Buffer's website explains the formula in detail, stating: "We don't want to have such a stark wage gap between team members in general. Even though a certain gap is inevitable and good, if someone in the same role, with similar experience, is making $100,000 less, that feels unfair in the grand scheme of things."

This transparency goes back to the importance of trust mentioned in Chapter 3. Today's workforce is rebelling against everything profitability was distorted to represent in the Industrial Era: distrust, oppression, and lack of concern for human capital.

As Paul put it, a talent-focused organization has a people strategy. That means rethinking pay and profitability. The bottom line now relies on how well you invest in your human capital—not just part of it, but all of it.

| Human Resources Strategy | People Strategy |
|---|---|
| Builds programs and processes to attract, retain, and motivate talent | Builds programs and processes to improve human performance |
| Measures and tracks productivity, engagement, and costs related to human capital | Develops and engages employees to improve organizational performance |
| Assumes leaders and employees will be accountable, doing what is necessary to help the organization reach its goals | Holds every employee accountable, maintaining communication and focus to ensure the organization reaches its goals |
| Supports the organization's business strategy | Drives the organization's business strategy |

## Make Change

In the Industrial Era, profits mattered and longevity was prevalent. In the Talent Economy, people matter and disruption is prevalent. This is changing how organizations think about talent, even for a company founded in 1845.

Considered to be the global leader in HR transformation, Deloitte's mission is to be Business Led, People Driven. Despite their research on human capital trends, Deloitte realized there was much they didn't know about the 60 percent of their workforce that's comprised of Millennials.

Deloitte's most recent employee research revealed new trends and ways in which the organization could improve its talent-focused initiatives.

For starters, "We expect and plan for some level of turnover," explained Mike Preston, Chief Talent Officer at Deloitte. The organization has come to realize that the largest percentage of its workforce is a generation that grew up being disrupted all the time. As a result, they aren't afraid of change, and even embrace it. Initially, Preston said Deloitte's leadership didn't like the idea of losing young professionals to turnover, but the organization has since learned that disruption is part of their reality, so they focus on leadership behaviors and values.

"We're in an open talent economy now, which means many employees will want to work in more than one job and for more than one company," Preston said. Rather than fight this reality, the organization has adapted to it.

"We're working to create a high-quality employee experience for them. We realize they are more likely to job-hop, but if we can create an engaging experience while they're here, they will be more loyal to our brand and more likely to work for us again or possibly be a client someday. We're not trying to keep them as employees for life, we're trying to make them colleagues for life."

Dr. Sydney Finkelstein is a professor of management at the Tuck Center for Leadership at Dartmouth College. He spent 10 years studying the world's greatest bosses across 18 industries, and surprisingly discovered these extraordinary leaders achieved outstanding results in large part because they abandoned conventional thinking about keeping the best employees. These leaders, most of whom were billionaires, weren't afraid to lose their best people. On the contrary, most willingly unleashed their top performers onto the world, even going out of their way to help them land outside opportunities.

These leaders believe a company is better off having the best people for a short time than average people forever, and they are uncompromising when it comes to recruiting. These leaders didn't want average; they wanted mind-blowing. They searched high and low for unusually talented individuals, often experimenting with nontraditional hires, and tolerating higher levels of churn when some of these hires didn't work out.

When a stream of top performers go on to better things, their departures usually hasten the flow of more top talent into the company. Renowned for having an outstanding boss, these organizations developed reputations as places to go to supercharge a career. High-potential prospects began flocking to these bosses and not their competitors, eager for a chance to train with the best.

Equally important, Dr. Finkelstein discovered that top performers keep delivering benefits for their employers, even when they stop working for the company. Great bosses build networks of former employees, turning to them for information, vendor relationships, and new recruits. They intuitively understand that every star who leaves the company makes the alumni network that much more powerful.

Accepting the "flow of talent," as Finkelstein puts it, makes an organization far more resilient, sustainable, and successful because its better tailored to many of today's realities, including volatile markets and disruption, and an entrepreneurial, gig economy that encourages frequent shifts in employment over the course of an individual's career.

In the Talent Economy, people are an organization's greatest asset. That means investing in and supporting their skill development, no matter where their careers may take them.

Deloitte has even gone so far as to shift its focus on "developing leaders not just for us, but for society," Preston said. "Millennials are holistic. They don't separate their personal life from their work life. It's not just about work-life balance. It's about work-life integration." As a result, Deloitte has started thinking about how to be a holistic company, positively influencing the well-being of employees. The firm has shifted its talent management practices to be a good steward to its employees, clients, and communities.

Furthermore, according to Deloitte's 2015 study of 3,726 Millennials, there are key differences between how Millennials define diversity and inclusion in comparison to other generations:

| Industrial Era (Boomer and Gen X) Definitions | Talent Economy (Millennials) |
|---|---|
| Define diversity in terms of demographics, equal opportunity, and physical characteristics | Define diversity as a mix of unique experiences, identities, ideas, and opinions |
| Define inclusion in terms of equity, fairness, and the integration, acceptance, and tolerance of gender, racial, and ethnic diversity | Define inclusion as teaming, valuing a culture of connectivity, and using collaborative tools to drive organizational impact |

In addition to being holistic, Deloitte's research revealed that Millennials practice cognitive diversity, viewing diversity as the blending of different backgrounds, experiences, and perspectives within a team. Here again, Deloitte is trying to be responsive and incorporate this same approach throughout the entire organization.

Deloitte's reinvestment in its changing workforce has reaped rewards. Preston said the firm's turnover is now at historic lows while engagement is at historic highs. Deloitte has continuously ranked among Great Places to Work, and employee rankings for trust, pride, and transparency have all inched up, plus Deloitte has observed improvements on their own employee surveys.

Deloitte continually reinvests in its employee relationships and has committed to being talent-centered, even amidst change. (As a company founded in 1845, Deloitte has seen its fair share of change.) Preston credit's Deloitte's CEO, a "staunch believer" in new talent strategies, for the firm's continued success. "Taking care of our team is the right thing to do and it's right for business," he said. By embracing disruption as the norm, the company has been able to stay relevant and competitive in a changing workforce.

## Own Disruption

Matthew Loyd's grandfather worked for Boeing for 40 years. He retired 30 years ago and is still living off his pension. Loyd said this era of "long arches" has come to an end, as in the length of time someone spends on a job, or with a single company, or retiring on pensions and social security. Long arches have been replaced with disruption, and success is now reliant on mission and vision.

Loyd has worked in lead marketing roles for several notable companies including Misfit, Gap, Method, and Clif Bar. Each of these companies are market leaders in their respective industries, and Loyd credits their success on having "social missions long before social missions were popular." Even when he worked for the Old Navy division of Gap, there was a mission to give access to great style to everyone, regardless of socio-economic background. At the time, providing fashion in an affordable price range was a game-changing concept.

Likewise, each of these companies had a "progressive vision of the future," readily willing to disrupt, innovate, and do something different. From Loyd's perspective, it's this combination of mission and vision which successfully engages employees, giving them a market advantage and placing them ahead of the competition.

"The very first rabid fan base, from a marketing standpoint, are your own employees," Loyd said. "Build the company the way it should be so that it provides the best possible employee environment. That's key." It's having a strong mission, a reason for being. That mission must be truthful and respectful to people, and it must bring everyone into the journey—not just the executive team. He noted the mission-vision imperative is the result of greedy corporations driving for profits for so long. Distrust is rampant, loyalty is over, and speed is enforcing change.

"This idea of transition is something that will only speed up. It will only become more dynamic. It will only continue to bewilder companies if they can't move," he said. Instead of seeing change as something that's inconvenient, he said organizations should figure out how to use it to their advantage. He even went so far as to say organizations should "own" disruption.

"We need organizations that say 'We're in the transition business now. We're going to pull in the best experts. We're going to build the curriculum. We're going to find the tools. We're going to build systems around things being in transition, rather than things around solid states that expire too quickly.' We have to be better at living in a state of flux," he said.

When the focus is on mission and vision, the flux part is easier to manage, because you are in conversation with your team, more responsive to their needs, and driven by something other than profits and traditions.

Long-arch thinking has fallen under scrutiny in many areas.

- *40-Hour Work Week*
  For example, some organizations are questioning the viability of the 40-hour work week in the Talent Economy. I recently met the owner of an engineering firm who said her entire team works between four and six hours per day. Now employees weren't worried about the time they needed to take off work to run errands, go to the dentist, or attend their children's school events. A shorter work day eliminated those distractions. Employees became more focused on their work, and productivity increased dramatically.

- *College Degrees*
  Others are questioning the viability of the lengthy pursuit of higher education in today's economy. Trista Harris, president of the Minnesota Council on Foundations, shared a story with me about a job applicant who had opted out of the traditional college track to take online courses in her field of interest from

six different colleges. Harris was immediately impressed with her creativity and drive. She didn't care that this person didn't have a degree, she was more impressed with her creative approach to obtaining an education.

- *Succession Planning*
  Loyd noted that some organizations remain devoted to the practice of succession planning and bench strength, which is practice based on Industrial Era-thinking where people worked 30–40 years at the same company and were promoted to executive roles. It's an example of "long-arch" thinking, and likely another practice that won't survive in a workforce that works in a state of flux.

Loyd said long arch thinking will stagnate organizations in today's economy and prevent them from gaining traction. He described it as a continual domino effect: grand plans are set, then knocked down because change happens. The next month, grand plans are set, and soon knocked down again. Much time is wasted trying to maintain business as usual, when it's anything but usual, and change continues to interfere with productivity and profitability.

## Invest in People

In the Industrial Era, skills were a competitive advantage, and sometimes the equivalent of survival. Those people who knew a trade were heavily sought after, given better job opportunities and often paid higher wages. People who didn't have skills could advance as long as they had intellect, which was acquired via access to education.

In the Talent Economy, skills and intellect still matter, but not as much as values and passion. In fact, Brandon Phipps, CEO, AcademicWorks, has grown a very successful business by hiring people for reasons that have little to do with their skills.

AcademicWorks has received numerous awards, most recently topping *Fortune*'s list of Best Small Workplaces in Tech. (In fact, the company received a perfect score, receiving 100 percent in employee ratings in each of the survey's 11 categories.) This small company comprised of 68 employees was also listed among the nation's 50 Best Workplaces for Camaraderie, for which more than 600 companies were nominated.

When I met Phipps at AcademicWorks' office in Austin, Texas, it was clear to see why the company is listed among the best workplaces. Phipps takes his company's mission, and the people who work to fulfill it, very seriously. This company definitely has a people strategy. AcademicWorks provides an online scholarship management platform for campuses and foundations. Since 2011, more than $660 million in scholarships have been awarded to more than 2 million students.

"We have to have a team that's really engaged in, and passionate about the work we do. This could be a student's only chance for a scholarship, so we must be obsessed with the customer experience," Phipps explained. For that reason, AcademicWorks hires based on a person's values, over their skills. Having a passion for the company's mission to help students access scholarships is imperative, and candidates must reflect the company's core values: Being Obsessed with Customer Experience, Engaged, Kind and Respectful.

Having the right personality and passion for the work isn't something that can be taught, whereas skills can, Phipps explained. "We want the people who will answer phone calls at 4:58 pm, and that's not something that can be taught."

The core values of service, kindness, and respect are evident throughout the entire organization. AcademicWorks is very intentional about relationship-building and dedicates a considerable amount of time to the process. Phipps described the "emotional tie" that sets the company apart from other organizations. Here are just a few ways they have built a talent-focused great place to work:

- New employees are assigned a buddy, responsible for introducing them to others within the company and answering questions about the culture, company, or market. The buddy also organizes a cross-departmental lunch so the new employee can meet team members from across the company;

- Employees are encouraged to take another employee from a different department out to lunch once per quarter on the company;

- A member of the executive team hosts a monthly lunch for the entire team, during which employees are invited to ask questions about the company;

- Members of the client services team receive a quarterly bonus based on customer satisfaction. The bonus is split between a cash component and a gift purchased by another team member (randomly assigned). The gift exchange provides an opportunity to team members to learn more about one another;

- The office closes an hour early on the first Friday of each month for a company happy hour, allowing employees time to interact in a social setting;

- On a quarterly basis, the executive team hosts a team meeting to review goals, disclose financials, and celebrate the team's achievements;

- On a weekly basis, the entire team receives an email tracking the team's progress on reaching their goals;

- Employees can submit compliments about other team members in confidential fashion into the Blue Box of Love. Submissions are read aloud in front of the entire company at quarterly team meetings;

- Employees receive a quarterly survey requesting feedback on company initiatives, such as the opportunity to review and rank two new employee benefits the company is considering adding; and

- Employees can submit ideas to the "It Would Be Great If..." box. One of the recommendations recently implemented was a request to add yoga classes.

As a Gen Xer, Phipps said his generation was taught "the wrong lesson" of not being vulnerable. "Younger generations are more vulnerable, and they are teaching us to lead with more emotion," he said. As a result, AcademicWorks seeks to be transparent, and readily admits and learns from failure.

Phipps said the company does everything in its power to avoid making people feel like "just another cog in the wheel." Turnover is virtually non-existent at AcademicWorks. In the six years since the company was founded, only seven employees have voluntarily left the company.

## Practice Empathy

When you put people first, radical changes occur. Gravity Payments, Deloitte, and AcademicWorks are all examples of companies that have seen positive results to the bottom line by being talent-focused and putting people first.

The Global Empathy Index published by *Harvard Business Review* seeks to identify which companies are successfully creating empathetic cultures. Why? Because it's been proven there is a direct link between empathy and profitability.

The Global Empathy Index ranks 170 companies on categories such as ethics, leadership, company culture, brand perception, public messaging through social media, CEO approval ratings from workers, ratio of women on boards, as well as accounting infractions and scandals. Information is drawn from a variety of sources, including S&P Capital IQ, Glassdoor, tweets posted on Twitter, and feedback from a panel of World Economic Forum's Young Global Leaders who are asked to rate the companies' morality.

When comparing 2015 to 2016, the top 10 companies in the Global Empathy Index increased in value more than twice as much as the bottom 10, and generated 50 percent more earnings (defined by market capitalization).

Among the more interesting findings:

- Five of the 10 most empathic companies are based in Silicon Valley (Facebook, Alphabet, LinkedIn, Netflix, Microsoft). They're also among the most profitable, making up for 15 percent of the index's total market capitalization, and the fastest growing companies. Their market capitalization grew by 23.3 percent in 2016 compared to a weighted average of 5.2 percent of all the companies in the index.

- British firms have been slow to recognize the direct correlation between corporate empathy and growth and productivity: 16 of the bottom 25 firms are traded on the London Stock Exchange. Also, U.S. banks scored 50 percent higher than UK ones.

Empathy is the cognitive and emotional understanding of others' experiences, which is important during this era of division between younger and older generations, and unparalleled political and social disruption.

Empathy is correlated with ethics, and any ethical failure can prove costly. This is evidenced by the drop in Wells Fargo's ranking, from 20 to 130, as a result of being under investigation for employees secretly creating millions of unauthorized bank and credit card accounts at the time of this book's printing.

In contrast, Facebook was named the most ethical company in 2016, owing to its focus on improving its internal culture and the introduction of the Empathy Lab, an engineering team devoted to accessibility on the mobile and desktop site for disabled users. In addition to physical disabilities, the team addresses technological ones, determining how to design Facebook for different parts of the world where screens may be smaller and the internet connections slower.

Turns out listening and responding skills outranked all others in producing the most successful leaders, according to a Development Dimensions International study of more than 15,000 leaders in 18 countries. Roughly 20 percent of employers in the United States now offer empathy training for managers.

Ford has taken the concept of putting yourself in someone else's shoes to a whole new level by having engineers wear a pregnancy-simulating belly garment so they can design vehicles with sensitivity to the extra weight, back pain, and bladder pressure that pregnant women experience getting in and out of cars.

How do you go about infusing your company culture with more empathy? According to The Empathy Business in London, start by identifying the trouble spots—the activities and behaviors that communicate a *lack* of empathy—and addressing those first.

Ryanair, headquartered in Dublin, Ireland, did this with its Always Getting Better (AGB) program, a company-wide initiative to improve all aspects of the customer experience. Under AGB, Ryanair scrapped unallocated seating, many hidden charges, and reduced carry-on luggage restrictions. The result was a net profit increase from €867 million in 2015 to €1.24 billion in 2016. The CEO infamously stated: "If I'd only known being nice to customers was going to work so well, I'd have started many years ago."

## Belonging and Purpose

Indeed, being nice to people—be it your customers or your employees—is important. Society had strayed so far from this concept in pursuit of the almighty dollar, we lost some of our humanity in the process. It's almost like we're going back to kindergarten, telling children to treat one another with respect and kindness on the playground. Nice should be the norm. It should be expected. People should be the priority, but often they are not. If your organization is sincere about employee engagement, it will go above and beyond being nice to deliver a sense of purpose and belonging.

I've researched belonging for several years now. I first noticed membership decline among younger generations when I worked for a membership organization in the late 1990s. Why weren't Gen Xers joining associations in the same way as Boomers? I was intrigued and determined to find out.

The study of generations presents powerful clues on where to start to faster connect with and influence people of different ages. Obviously, there are many factors that go into shaping an individual's experience, which is why everyone is unique. However, on the whole, those within a generation often exhibit surprisingly similar characteristics—and one of those characteristics shared by younger generations is the decline in membership involvement.

The challenge of engaging younger generations really started garnering attention in the 2000s, first apparent among membership associations. As Generation X came of age (1965-1981), it became increasingly obvious that engagement was changing and the change was tied to the shift in demographics.

After all, membership decline wasn't happening across the board with every generation. We weren't reading headlines about Baby Boomers suddenly up and leaving their beloved associations. Rather, there were countless reports of associations struggling to engage younger members. Consider the following timeline:

### 2000

Robert Putnam's book, *Bowling Alone: The Collapse and Revival of American Community,* cited data showing an aggregate decline in membership of traditional civic organizations, supporting his thesis that U.S. social capital had also declined.

### 2004

Declining membership became an urgent and highly publicized concern for all types of membership organizations. Media all over the world were covering stories about declining membership in everything from trade unions to scouting, churches, and veteran organizations.

### 2005

The *Journal of Association Leadership* explored the disappearance of the traditional association member base, classified as a white 50- to 60-year-old homeowner, upper educated, urban-based, married, and with a higher-level job. The article urged associations to prepare for rapidly approaching, significant demographic shifts.

### 2006

*The Washington Post* reported on declining membership engagement among Generation X. The article cited research that projected Xers would likely be interested in joining associations when they hit their peak earning years, but cautioned their participation was definitely "not a sure thing" because they wanted tangible services and real evidence that joining something is good for their careers.

*2010*

National Public Radio reported on the robust history of trade associations in America, citing the fact that during the past 10 years many had struggled to survive.

*2011*

At the annual meeting of the American Sociological Association, information was shared from a research project examining the overall decline in active memberships in civic groups, fraternal organizations, and other local associations since 1994. Research revealed that active membership had declined 6 percent; "generational differences" was cited as one of the reasons.

*2012*

The U.S. Chamber of Commerce Foundation published *The Millennial Generation Research Review,* announcing 62 percent of professional associations were experiencing flat or declining membership, the greatest challenge being engaging the membership of younger generations.

*2014*

Pew Research's *Millennials in Adulthood* study noted this generation has fewer attachments to traditional institutions.

What happened with membership associations was a preview into what would happen in the workforce. In recent years, there have been countless articles written and studies conducted to try to pinpoint why employee turnover among Millennials is skyrocketing. This isn't a fluke or something that will suddenly correct itself. This isn't just a phase and all this generational talk isn't just a lot of hot air with no real ramifications.

This denial has led to complacency and apathy and organizations have found themselves stuck in a rut of delivering the same old programs, focusing on the same old issues, generating the same old knowledge, planning the same old conference, and managing in the same old way.

Meanwhile, the leadership bemoans the fact that engagement is declining, that "kids today" have no concept of loyalty, and that the world is surely going to hell in a handbasket. There's a reason why disengagement is happening, and it's because the needs, interests, expectations, and values of younger generations are considerably different than the generations that have come before them.

Industrial Era organizations and practices simply won't inspire or engage the generations raised in a Talent Economy. Disengagement is happening because younger generations feel like they don't belong. Belonging, by definition, means you have a sense of ownership and a secure relationship. You feel empowered as an individual and an important and valued part of a team all at the same time. AcademicWorks delivers on this concept beautifully. Employees are empowered to make decisions, serve others, and voice their opinions (ownership), and they are continually appreciated, recognized and valued by other members of the team (relationship).

There's a lot of emphasis on purpose when it comes to engaging Millennial employees. I don't disagree with this, but I think belonging is often overlooked. Belonging is the meat and potatoes of employee engagement. Purpose is the gravy. Sometimes purpose is mistaken as something that can be resolved with the launch of a service project. Indeed, 84 percent of Millennials volunteer annually. So it's widely believed that if an organization dedicates a day to working on a Habitat for Humanity project, its Millennial employees will be more engaged.

This isn't the case.

Purpose is the feeling you are making a difference. Purpose is looking at what you've accomplished and feeling proud. But purpose isn't something an organization can accomplish in a single day or even a week. Purpose has to exist in the everyday, the mundane, and the routine.

In the Industrial Era, work was something you did from 9:00 to 5:00. You punched in and out of your job, and it was acceptable to dislike your job because it often resembled little more than a paycheck. The theory was that as long as you worked hard, you would get paid well, and then you could buy yourself a great house or boat or vacation and enjoy the good life on the weekends. But that era is over.

In the Talent Economy, most jobs are mobile. You can work whenever, wherever, and your ideas, innovation, and talent are valuable. And there's this shared sentiment that in a world rocked by violence and change and recession, you should spend time doing something you like to do. Life is short and YOLO (you only live once). Therefore, work has morphed into something resembling more of a hobby than a job, in that it's part of your identity and it brings you joy and pride.

Purpose is knowing that each and every day, the work you do is making a difference to someone, somewhere—possibly even yourself. Purpose is feeling proud of your accomplishments, the work you do, and the work your company does. Purpose is another way society is rebelling against the Industrial Era, because purpose is the refusal to work for an organization just so it can make more money and pay its CEOs 275 times more than the employees. Purpose blatantly asks: "How will I feel about working here?" When companies do a lousy job of delivering on purpose, the outcome can be toxic.

A friend of mine works for a renowned NASDAQ traded company, and he complains often about the work environment. In fact, the company was listed among the Worst Companies to Work For, which is something he is quick to point out. When I asked why he continues to work there, he said the pay is just too good. Yes, there are still people who will tolerate being miserable in exchange for a high salary.

But this is becoming less of the norm, especially among Millennials. And it comes at a high price to the company, literally and figuratively.

I guarantee that my friend, and other disgruntled and disengaged employees like him, aren't giving their best at work. He doesn't care about the company's well-being, and I seriously doubt he cares much about the people he's managing. This guy is just doing the minimum to get by, keep his job, and collect his check. In the meantime, he voices his frustration and spreads negativity about the company to everyone and anyone. Money can't buy happiness. Well, not unless you run the company like Dan Price.

## The Price Is Right

If Price would have only raised the minimum wage for his team, not taken a pay cut himself, and not focused on being a talent-focused organization, his $70,000 experiment would have likely failed. Employee engagement has little to do with compensation and everything to do with getting employees to care about the company and the work they do. It's valuing your people above everything else not just in a matter of speaking, but a matter of doing.

Dale Partridge, founder of StartUp Camp and author of *People Over Profit*, encourages organizations to ask themselves: What are we doing simply because of tradition? His book preaches the importance of putting people first, and it's written from experience.

Sevenly, an online apparel company Partridge founded in 2011, has generated more than $25 million in revenue. Because the company donates $7 for every purchased item on the site, Sevenly has contributed more than $4.2 million to a variety of nonprofits and causes.

Staying true to its people-first model, at Sevenly the way employees are fired is similar to how they are hired. While many companies have security escort dismissed employees out of the building, Sevenly takes a different approach. Fired employees are invited back the following week to receive affirmation from their colleagues and a letter of recommendation. This practice might seem foolish, bizarre, or uncomfortable, but it just goes to show that truly talent-focused organizations will carefully consider every interaction with every person, prioritizing their needs and treating them with respect no matter what the situation. Partridge and Price are blazing the trail in the Talent Economy, engaging employees and making a positive difference. But there's still work to be done.

In 2016, *Harvard Business Review* published a list of the Best-Performing CEOs in the World. Interviews with the top three CEOs echoed themes of the talent-focused shift.

- Lars Rebien Sørensen, CEO of Novo Nordisk, a global healthcare company headquartered in Denmark, said the wide disparity between executive compensation and workers' compensation is creating a barrier to the employee passion and engagement, leading to greater distrust and creating challenges for organizations.

- Martin Sorrell, CEO of WPP, a British multinational advertising and public relations company, said too many CEOs have been in their roles for too long, becoming more conservative over time. He admitted he is taking fewer risks than he did when he was younger, but he does recognize the need to be purpose-driven and is moving towards keeping people and purpose at the center of the business.

- Pablo Isla, CEO of Inditex, the largest fashion group in the world headquartered in Spain, said he's gradually learning to be less rational and more emotional. "Motivating people and generating a sense of spirit inside a company are essential parts of the CEO's role. We need to appeal to our employees' emotions to help create an environment where they can innovate," he stated. He's also focused on maintaining an entrepreneurial spirit within the company to help navigate change. This means fewer meetings and formal presentations, replacing them with more feedback and empowering others to make decisions.

Many organizations are straddling the Industrial Era and Talent Economy, trying to transition toward new thinking and methodologies. It isn't easy, but it does pay off.

Price shares via video the story of an executive at Yahoo! who took an 80 percent payout to work at Gravity Payments, making the switch to "serve our mission" and to have an opportunity to help and serve others. A Gravity Payments' employee blogged about the work experience, and the company-wide focus on purpose. An excerpt of the blog follows.

> When asking our Merchant Relations Specialist how he stays motivated day-to-day, he said, "I am intrinsically motivated to work through the relationships I have developed with the small business owners I help every day."...
>
> Part of the way we foster intrinsic motivation is removing extrinsic motivators that might otherwise distract us from our lives.
>
> A major distraction for most people is rent. If we're living paycheck-to-paycheck, that stressor will always be at the forefront of our minds. It may cause us to cut corners or not fully focus on the task at hand. At Gravity, we pay a living wage to ensure our colleagues can live comfortably without worrying about where the money for their next meal will come from. ...
>
> Our CEO, Dan Price, encourages our team to use intrinsic motivation to power our lives, so we can look at our jobs as

an extension of our values, and not a place we go to make ends meet.[1]

Clearly, when you put people first, your organization will be capable of making more than just a profit.

---

1 Reprinted with permission. Copyright Gravity Payments. August 24, 2016. https://gravitypayments.com/highlights/youredistracting-stop-now-unleash-full-potential/

**CHAPTER SUMMARY**

Being truly talent-focused means prioritizing your people above all else—even money. It's important to be aware of your organization's pay structure and to question whether it's negatively affecting employee engagement, morale, or motivation. When money is no longer the company's sole focus and people become the priority, many positive outcomes occur. The organizations that put people first are responsive to employee needs, resilient and capable of change, experience less turnover, positively contribute to their communities, and observe greater profitability overall.

**QUESTIONS TO CONSIDER**

1. When did I last say "thank you" to my team?

2. Do I make promises to my team but fail to keep them because I'm "too busy?"

3. Is it important to me that the organization I work for values people more than profit? Why or why not?

4. What changes need to be made in our organization to build better relationships and foster teamwork?

5. What holds our organization back from putting people first?

6. Belonging, by definition, means you have a sense of ownership and a secure relationship. Who among our employees, volunteers, and members are most likely to feel like they belong? How could we improve our relationships and give more ownership to those who feel like they don't belong?

*The Talent Generation model relies on two key components: putting people first and maintaining a future-focus. Being future-focused means the organization won't risk aging out or becoming irrelevant or stagnant because it will always be prepared for who and what comes next.*

**Build the Future**
Education and Business Align

**Leadership**
Passion, Optimism, Humility, Urgency

**Collaborate**
Innovation via Team-Building

**Acceptance**
Inclusion and Trust

**Future Focus**
Research, Trends, Opportunities

**People First**
Mission, Vision, and Strategy

*"If you don't think about and plan for the future, then your organization has no future."*

JACOB MORGAN

CHAPTER 5
. . . . . . . . . . . . . . . . . . . . . . . . . . . .
# Future Focus

Sometimes I wonder what my reaction would have been if, as a 20-something starting out at Price Waterhouse nearly three decades ago, I had been magically transported to today's PwC.

I would have been stunned by how much had changed.

During most of my career at the firm, the rewards system focused more on quantity than quality of work, although clients demanded standards just as high then as the ones they do now. Bigger bonuses and promotions went to those who sacrificed more of their personal lives, whereas our current HR policies primarily reward quality, and value the work and life needs of every person.

The Millennials among my colleagues emphasize finding satisfaction in their jobs and are willing to be vocal about what they want from a career and a company. They're also extremely globally oriented—they know and care much more about what's going on all over the world than I did at their age. And they're adept at leveraging technological advances to be more flexible.

But most of all, I would have been astonished that PwC's Millennials don't only demand to know the organization's purpose—its reason for being—but are prepared to leave the firm if that purpose doesn't align with their own values.

When I was coming up, we knew what we were doing, but we didn't ask why we did it. We didn't give much thought to our, or the firm's, role in society. For me, that point crystallizes the generational issues that PwC and many other organizations are facing as they hire greater numbers of Millennials.[1]

In 2014, Bob Moritz, the U.S. Chairman and Senior Partner of PwC, published an article in *Harvard Business Review* sharing that despite the fact that PwC hires as many as 8,000 new college graduates each year, "I didn't realize how little I really knew about these young people in the workforce." Moritz admits he didn't comprehend the "very real generational differences" that existed in his own workforce until PwC collaborated with researchers from the University of Southern California and London Business School.

His article served as a wake-up call to his peers, elaborating on how PwC had shifted its talent practices to be inclusive of younger professionals and urging other companies to take the time to understand Millennials and devise an effective people strategy.

I admire Mortiz's willingness to admit he made assumptions and didn't really take the time to get to know Millennials. I appreciate his effort to call on other executives to follow suit, but here we are three years later and the talent conundrum hasn't improved in the slightest.

Which leads me to question: How much time have leaders spent getting to know their younger colleagues? How much do they really know about this generation—and how much do they just *guess*?

---

1 Copyright 2014. Harvard Business Review. Reprinted with permission.
  https://hbr.org/2014/11/the-us-chairman-of-pwc-on-keeping-millennials-engaged

The fact is, if we're not engaged in building relationships with the youngest generations in our workforce, we can't effectively engage them, nor can we plan our future. In this rapidly changing, disruption-is-the-norm workforce, we must focus on the future, or our organizations and economy risks getting left behind.

## Knowing Y (aka Millennials)

I highlighted several employee engagement obstacles in the last chapter, but there are other obstacles prohibiting us from engaging talent, young talent specifically. Generation Y (1982–1995), also known as Millennials, came of age during a time of economic recession, digital innovation, and political revolution. They are the first generation of the Post-Industrial Era. All too often we refer to this change as being purely driven by technology, but that's not the case at all.

In fact, in 2014 I authored a book on this generation titled *Knowing Y: Engage the Next Generation Now* (ASAE). The book identifies five currents of change that are so powerful they have been referred to as mini-economies within the Talent Economy. The Sharing, Gig, Knowledge, Experience, and Impact economies are spurring unprecedented social, economic, and political change on a global scale.

Not surprising, these economies have shaped the opinions, values, and behaviors of Generation Y in radical ways—which will undoubtedly shape *every* generation's opinions, values, and behaviors and have already begun to do so. It's the Trickle-Up Effect. Sooner or later, the youngest generation influences the older generations, and this is how widespread change often occurs.

The arrival of the Millennial generation is closely aligned with many powerful economic transitions. I seriously doubt the arrival of a single generation has ever ushered in this much transition at any other time in history. There is much to learn from this generation and much potential that has yet to be tapped.

All these emerging economies simply point to the volume of change that's occurring in every aspect of how we live, work, and do business—and further support the fact that the generation that's come of age in this era of change is considerably different than the generations that came before.

## Experience Economy

Walt Disney World offers an experience, as do Apple Stores, Cirque du Soleil, the Geek Squad, Dave and Buster's, American Girl, TED Conferences, and Chuck E. Cheese. Some economists believe experiences have emerged as the most valuable commodity.

Experiences create value and a competitive advantage in an over-saturated market. Buyers of experiences value being engaged by what the company reveals over the duration of time. Experiences are more memorable and considered more valuable than goods and services. Experiences can offer enjoyment, knowledge, diversion, beauty, change, and access. Experiences affect who we are, what we can accomplish, and where we are going. And now there is proof that when companies invest in the employee experience, they are more productive and profitable.

Decades ago nobody cared about the employee experience because all the power was in the hands of employers. Employers simply needed to list a job and provide people a place to do that job. Nothing else really mattered. There was no focus on engagement, inspiration, empowerment, designing beautiful workplaces, using modern technology, or the like. These things have just recently become mainstream topics of discussion.

Why? Because the power has now shifted into the hands of employees. Organizations have always assumed that they can create a place where people *needed* to work, and now they realize they must create a place where people *want* to work.

The war for talent has never been so fierce. People are turning to non-traditional ways of earning a living such as creating products on Etsy, renting out their homes on Airbnb, driving for Uber or Lyft, becoming freelancers on sites like Upwork, and the like. Technology platforms such as Linkedin have also made it incredibly easy for head hunters to steal talent from their competitors. In this Talent Economy what can organizations do to help make sure that employees want to show up? Focus on the employee experience.

Jacob Morgan is the author of *The Employee Experience Advantage,* for which he researched the employee experience—defined as culture, physical space, and technology—at organizations around the world.

- *Culture*

  The cultural environment is the one that you feel; it's the vibe you get when you walk in the door and it's the mood and the tone that the workplace sets. It's the leadership style, the sense of purpose your employees feel, the organizational structure, and the people that make up your organization. It's not written and it's not stated, yet it is one of the most important elements of creating and designing the employee experience.

- *Physical Space*

  The physical workspace is the one we can see, touch, taste, and smell. It's the art that hangs on the walls, the office floor plan, the demographics of the people we work with, and any physical perks we might access such as an on-site gym, café, or lounge area. The most progressive companies have a physical space that reflects the organization's culture and adapts to multiple modes of working in the Talent Economy, allowing for mobility, and providing areas designated to focus, collaboration, learning, and socializing.

- *Technology*

  The technological environment of an organization refers to the tools employees use to get their jobs done. Morgan refers to technology as the central nervous system of the organization. This includes everything from the internal social network your company might use to the mobile devices that are approved, to the organization's laptops, desktops, video conferencing solutions, apps, software, and other tech tools. This is an area that's constantly updating and evolving and influencing the employee experience. Big data, wearable devices, the internet of things, collaboration tools, robots, and automation are all technology developments organizations should seek to understand.

Morgan analyzed 252 companies around the world, including those listed among *Fortune*'s Best Companies to Work. He developed 17 variables to measure, then hired a team of researchers who ranked the companies based on publicly available information on each company: Glassdoor data, Google searches, and more. The team ranked each organization based on their competencies in the culture, technology, and physical space categories.

The companies that ranked the highest in all three categories Morgan refers to as Experiential Organizations. "These are the companies doing an amazing job at creating employee experiences. In other words, they are awesome at technology, awesome at culture, and awesome at physical space." However, Morgan's research revealed that only 15 companies were investing in all three areas; only 6 percent of the 252 companies are excelling at employee experience.

Some of the companies are ones you would expect to find on the list, like Google and Facebook. Industrial-Era companies like Cisco, Microsoft, and Accenture also made the list. "Some of these companies have been around for a long time, so this is not just a young Silicon Valley thing," Morgan noted.

Moreover, Morgan analyzed the Experiential Organizations against several business metrics. This is where it gets really interesting.

- *Lists*

  Morgan reviewed numerous published lists, ranging from customer satisfaction to most innovative, best places to work, most diverse, greenest, and smartest companies. "It turns out that the Experiential Organizations appear on all these lists far more often than any other type of company," he said. "Sometimes 10 times more often."

- *Profitability*

  Morgan's research revealed that the Experiential Organizations have higher average revenue per employee, profit per employee, and higher employee tenure. "These companies are actually smaller than other categories of companies. In other words, their revenue and their profits are higher but they are able to do so by having fewer people. So they are more productive," he said.

- *Stock*

  Morgan created fictitious stock portfolios of the 15 Experiential Organizations and compared them against the other 237 companies he had initially researched. "I compared it against the S&P 500, the NASDAQ, and the Experiential Organizations far out performed everybody else. That to me was a very clear sign that investing in these areas has clear financial impact."

I toured JL Buchanan's (JLB) office while researching this book. JL Buchanan is a retail consulting firm based in Minneapolis which specializes in getting brands into Target stores. To Morgan's point, JL Buchanan made a switch two years ago, completely revamping its physical space to incorporate the company's brand and engage employees in an experience, and it has yielded beneficial results.

The company is a results-oriented work environment (ROWE), meaning that employees can work where and when they want to work as long as they are achieving measurable results. (More on ROWE in the next section). In other words, employees don't have to come into the office and can work virtually, but since the redesign, more employees are working on-site than before. "With ROWE your office really doesn't matter. The office is a tool. It's a place that you don't have to be. We used to be in cube-land two years ago, and while it's always been optional for people to come in to work, we have more people come in now than we ever did," said Lana Jones, Vice President of Talent and Culture at JL Buchanan.

When the company decided to redesign its office space, it wasn't just a matter of switching out the carpet or adding new lighting. JL Buchanan's CEO challenged the team to design the office of the future. With 68 percent of the team being Millennials, the space had to reflect their style of working. The company also wanted clients to feel welcome to "set up shop here and work;" Target's headquarters is located nearby, so creating a space where people would want to gather and collaborate was important, Jones said. For that reason, JL Buchanan's workplace is designed more like a home than an office. There is no receptionist; rather a large foyer with chandelier and moss wall greet you in the entryway, with a coatroom on your right.

Every aspect of the design was intentional. Removing the receptionist not only encourages the team to personally greet their guests, it's also representative of the company's commitment to reducing unnecessary costs. The moss wall is a nod to the company's commitment to sustainability, but also gives employees a therapeutic space. (They can spritz the wall with water when they are feeling stressed.) And a closer look at the chandelier reveals an intricate design of sculptures representing people. "It's a signature piece. We're all about our team here, so the chandelier is representative of the collective spirit of JLB and the talent that we have," Jones said.

A large wall, running most of the length of the office, was crafted by an artist in New York. It features 200 pieces of individually stamped concrete. As you walk down the hall, the design starts out extremely jagged and progressively becomes smoother. The wall also features different color tones: look at it from one direction and it's red, look at it from another direction and it's gray. Jones said the wall's jagged construction represents that clients come to JLB with challenges, and JLB "paves the way for them," making it into a smooth, streamlined process. The wall's color scheme represents JLB can see "both sides of a relationship," bringing companies together in mutually beneficial ways.

There is no assigned seating in this workspace. No one has a desk or an office. There are no filing cabinets. The entire office is paperless. When people arrive at work, they grab their bin, which is about the size of a shoebox and includes any personal items they want to keep at work. For most people, this includes a family photo and cords for their laptops and mobile devices, Jones said. They then pick a place they want to work for the day. The office is open, comprised of large meeting rooms with glass walls, a café, and a large open space with tables, booths, and chairs. The open environment is designed to break down walls—literally—between roles and departments, thereby eliminating hierarchy and encouraging collaboration.

"This was a big transition," Jones said, recalling the transition from an office reliant on paperwork, desks, and clutter to one that's open and designed for mobility. She said the exercise forced the entire company to focus on what's important and to simplify processes, while incorporating technology and eliminating paperwork.

Making an intentional switch from the old world to the new world has made a positive difference at JLB. The new environment has fostered more collaboration, productivity, and boosted morale. "I'm very proud of the space that we have because I think it truly walks the talk. It reflects the culture we have, it reflects the way we work and that speaks volumes," Jones said.

## Gig Economy

"What do you do?" used to be a simple question. Individuals defined themselves by profession: teacher, engineer, pilot or by company: IBM, NASA, Kodak. But it was always one job, one identity. Today's young professionals, however, aren't as easily categorized. They struggle to prioritize which job title to place on their LinkedIn profiles. They tend to work several jobs simultaneously and this tendency toward multi-careerism—referred to as the Gig Economy or "sidepreneurism"—is taking over the workforce.

In the Gig Economy, we can expect more part-time team opportunities, a workforce that desires flexibility, plus a healthy work-life balance, increased ability to parent, and time to pursue additional education or a side hustle.

Multi-careerism is ridding the world of silos, titles, and roles. Add to that the widespread demand for flextime, mobility, and the fact that Millennials have launched a record number of start-up businesses, one can quickly surmise that the world of work isn't about working 9 to 5 anymore. The entire workforce is moving into an entrepreneurial mindset, both figuratively and literally.

Prior to this generation's arrival, there was an order in life: finish your education, get a job, get married, buy a house, have children. The Millennial generation doesn't do things in any one order. They do what feels right, feel less pressure to succeed using the traditional career path, and choose jobs where they feel they can make a difference.

Young adults taking on jobs are seeking opportunities that allow them to prioritize their own time. And with Millennials making up the largest percentage of the workforce, their desires for more autonomy, mobility, and gigs will drive future organizational behavior—indeed, they already have.

## ROWE

As the world of silos, titles, and roles disappears, autonomy emerges in its place. ROWE is a perfect example of a Gig-inspired workforce program.

Jody Thompson and Cali Ressler built ROWE on the premise that if every person in the organization is guided by measurable results and given the autonomy to achieve those results, it would radically change the employer-employee relationship.

Not to be confused with flexibility, in a ROWE, each person is 100 percent accountable and 100 percent autonomous. Managers manage the work, not the people. Employees are clear about what their measurable results are and empowered to do what they need to do to get the job done. "No results, no job," Thompson explained.

Thompson and Ressler developed and tested their ROWE theory out while working in the HR department at Best Buy in 2004. "Lo and behold, it was extremely successful! Engagement scores went up and productivity went up, but at a much higher level than with flexibility. It was pure management innovation," Thompson said.

She and Ressler shared the results of their experiment with the executive team, and in 2005 Best Buy made headlines with its official introduction of ROWE. The program, which was then described as "TiVo for your work" was lauded as a next generation HR strategy. Best Buy's corporate employees no longer needed to punch a clock, they would be measured by results, and could work whenever, wherever. ROWE reportedly helped Best Buy save $2.2 million over three years, reducing turnover 90 percent and increasing productivity by 41 percent.

Despite these amazing results, the big box retailer once again made headlines in 2013 when it decided to reverse ROWE and return to a mandatory eight-hour, on-site work day. Earlier that same year, Yahoo! CEO Melissa Mayer axed the company's telecommuting program. Both companies were experiencing financial decline and believed a return to traditional workforce management was necessary. Thompson and Ressler strongly disagreed. They responded by writing a blog post to Best Buy, which was covered by national media. Here's an excerpt:

> While we agree that Best Buy must take drastic measures to turn their business around, moving back to a 20th century, paternalistic "command and control" environment is most certainly not the answer. ... They are sending a clear message that they are more concerned with having leadership excel at monitoring the hallways, rather than building a leadership team that excels at defining clear, measurable results, and holding people accountable for achieving those results.

Likewise, Thompson and Ressler's open letter to Mayer was covered by national media. Here's an excerpt from that post:

> We don't think you deliberately meant to send a message to Yahoo! employees that you are an Industrial Age dictator that prefers to be a babysitter vs. a 21st century CEO that can lead a company into the future. Or did you? ... Last week, you didn't just mess up. You dug yourself a hole that no one can see to the bottom of. You made a move that has effectively painted you as 2013's CEO Who Doesn't Get It. And we might as well just give that award to you right now for the next 7 years, because what you've done has sealed your place at the top of that list for a very long time.

Whether you agree with Thompson and Ressler's viewpoint, it's hard to deny the track record of ROWE's success, and it's easy to understand why its founders would be shocked at the retreat to more traditional management models.

Based on years of research and ROWE consulting, Thompson has observed companies struggling to engage talent because they are directionless and mired in power struggles. She sees employers fixated on how and where the work is done rather than what work is being accomplished and why. She sees teams moving in different directions, doing activities that cost a lot of resources, money, and effort, and managers who reward their employees for showing up early or working late. "We're so focused on all the wrong things," Thompson said.

Of course, all this goes against the grain of the Millennials, raised in the Talent Economy with entrepreneurial mindsets and a strong desire to work where they can make a difference. When the mission is confusing or interrupted by people micro-managing how you spend your time, young people often disengage.

Autonomy, on the other hand, makes everyone in the company feel like a CEO: trusted, important and unencumbered. At the same time, everyone feels like they are part of a team, being coached and learning how to master what they're doing. "To me, that's the definition of engagement," she said.

"The way people are going to work and need to work in this information age is different. The way that kids are growing up today and how they communicate and collaborate and work and play and live is different. We're holding ourselves back by not embracing change." Autonomy taps into the Millennials' desire to feel empowered at their place of work.

At Nordstrom, employees are given a single card that says: Use good judgment in all situations. "We encourage our employees to work as though it's their name on the door, to build their own business and do what they feel is right to build lasting relationships with their customers," stated Mary Porter, Director of HR at Nordstrom, in an interview with *Business Insider.* Shortly after introducing the card in 2014, Porter reported the company observed increased employee morale and retention, especially among Millennials.

Nordstrom also encourages its employees to use their "good judgement" in an ongoing effort to build up the employee community, encouraging people they think would be good Nordstrom employees to pursue job opportunities with the retailer.

"When Nordstrom employees are out in the community getting a coffee, having dinner or purchasing something at another place of business, they are encouraged to make connections with those who offer the service we are looking for with hopes that they may consider a career with Nordstrom," stated Porter. This, once again, plays into the Millennial desire to feel empowered by their employers.

**Holocracy**

In 2015, Zappos' CEO Tony Hsieh announced the company would switch to a self-managed enterprise without "people managers" or titles. Those who held manager titles at the online shoe and clothing company were invited to either leave with severance or find new roles in the company that suited their talents and interests, but no longer would they have authority over anyone else. Instead, authority would be distributed across "circles" and the roles they fill within those circles. This management practice is called Holacracy. It replaces top-down management by distributing power, and was designed to allow for rapid evolution in the core processes of an organization.

Hsieh explained his decision to move to Holocracy in an employee memo:

> Research shows that every time the size of a city doubles, innovation or productivity per resident increases by 15 percent. But when companies get bigger, innovation or productivity per employee generally goes down. So we're trying to figure out how to structure Zappos more like a city, and less like a bureaucratic corporation. In a city, people and businesses are self-organizing. We're trying to do the same thing by switching from a normal hierarchical structure to

a system called Holacracy, which enables employees to act more like entrepreneurs and self-direct their work instead of reporting to a manager who tells them what to do.

Holacracy is the brainchild of Brian Robertson, a former programmer and entrepreneur. As he was growing a software company he started in 2001, Robertson realized the management-hierarchy system wasn't agile or adaptable, and didn't allow employees to effectively contribute and use their talent. He developed his own management approach, Holacracy, in 2007 to combat these challenges. More than 300 companies are using Holacracy but Zappos, at 1,000 employees, is the largest.

An organization operating as a Holacracy takes powers traditionally reserved for executives and managers and spreads them to all employees. Circles are a key element of Holacracy, each with a designated "lead link" appointed to guide a given circle to fulfill its stated purpose. Typically, the circle structure looks like this:

- **Anchor Circle:** Board of Directors.

- **General Company Circle (GCC):** Traditional executive leadership of the company. It is the only sub-circle in the Anchor circle.

- **Sub-Circle:** Dedicated to specific functions of a company, like marketing and production.

- **Roles:** An element of a traditional job broken down into a task. A marketing circle, for example, can contain roles like social media, advertising, web marketing, and brand development. Every role comes with agreed-upon accountabilities. If a role's responsibilities become too much for just one person to take care of, then it can expand into a new sub-circle with its own roles. A role is not representative of a person. A single employee can have many roles, and roles are always subject to change.

Two highly structured meetings are also a trademark of Holacracy. The formality of the meetings is meant to streamline the decision-making process, reduce the number of daily interactions regarding decisions, and eliminate time-sucking meetings with low yield.

Governance Meetings are usually held once a month to refine the circle's operating structure. The recommended meeting process is as follows:

1. **Check-in Round:** One at a time, each participant has space to call out distractions and orient to the meeting.

2. **Administrative Concerns:** Quickly address any logistical matters, such as time allotted for the meeting and any planned breaks.

3. **Agenda Building:** Participants add agenda items, using just one or two words per item. Each agenda represents one tension to process. (Tensions are defined as a person's sense that there is a gap between the current reality and a potential future.) Facilitator captures agenda items and the tension in a list.

4. **Integrative Decision-Making Process:** Each agenda item is addressed, one at a time. The proposer speaks uninterrupted then others weigh in, one at a time.

5. **Closing Round:** Once the agenda is complete or the meeting is nearing its scheduled end, the facilitator gives each person space to share a closing reflection about the meeting.

Tactical Meetings are held weekly to ensure each circle member is on the same page and to address any problems hampering progress. The recommended meeting process is as follows:

1. **Check-in Round:** Each person has an uninterrupted chance to mention anything on their mind.

2. **Checklist Review:** Facilitator reads aloud a checklist for each of the roles, which the person in question responds to either with "check" or "no check."

3. **Metrics Review:** Each role responsible for a data report shares a briefing on it.

4. **Progress Updates:** The facilitator reads aloud each project, asking, "Any updates?" The project lead either says "no updates" or gives a brief explanation.

5. **Agenda Building:** Each person has a chance to raise a tension, represented only by one or two words.

6. **Triage Issues:** Facilitator gives each person with a tension a chance to explain their issue and discuss it with other members. Facilitator determines what next steps need to be taken to resolve the issue as quickly as possible.

7. **Closing Round:** Each person has an uninterrupted chance to share a closing reflection about the meeting.

In addition, it is recommended Strategy Meetings are held every six months to review the circle's overall progress and develop long-term goals. There is no mandated structure but it is recommended these meetings last four or more hours.

In an interview with CNN Money, Alexis Gonzales-Black, member of Zappos' Holacracy Transition Team, said the switch to holocracy is radical, yet rewarding. "Managers are really responsible for two separate things. One is being the technical advisor for their work and the other is the people-management or people development. And we all know of a manager that's been promoted because they are a great individual contributor, but may not necessarily be a great people person or people developer. In holocracy we can split those two roles apart," she explained.

Each circles' lead link is accountable for setting priorities and metrics for that circle. That's where the technical advisor side of management resides. The people-development is moved elsewhere— to a circle which is entirely dedicated to people-development.

"The People-People Circle is a group of folks who are really passionate about professional development," Gonzales-Black explained. Former managers aren't assigned to former employees for professional development, "so you know you're getting somebody new to help you and professionally develop you," she added.

Productivity is the core benefit of Holacracy, as well as employee engagement via autonomy. "When you distribute authority and you make sure people take ownership over their work, and you're not busy overseeing the work of other people, it frees up (a manager's) capacity so you can do all those projects on your list that you just haven't had the time to do," Gonzales-Black stated. "We're asking managers to distribute authority to their teams and to get rid of their titles which is an incredible ask, but we're also asking team members to step up and take ownership over their work in a way that maybe they haven't before."

Since the decision to move to holacracy, Zappos has faced a lot of criticism and spurred debate—much like the ROWE concept. *Fortune* magazine covered Zappos' transition to holacracy in-depth in 2016, reporting on all that has gone well with the transition (achieving its highest operating profits ever in 2015) and all that has proven challenging (trying to decipher compensation and a performance review process), summarizing:

> The result has been an epic clash between a doctrinaire
> set of rules and a culture whose very essence has been a
> tolerance for the unruliness that comes with individual
> self-expression. Holacracy has empowered some people and
> hamstrung others. The company's most utopian dreams,

which include banishing internal politics, have not yet been realized.

The article noted the Hsieh isn't concerned about the critics. As Zappos grew, he saw the company become more bureaucratic and lose some of its spark and he's "absolutely sure" the future is about self-management.

"This is an opportunity to become a more innovative, agile company. One that doesn't suffer from the problems of bureaucracy, and politics and is more open to change—and that's a risk that we're willing to take," Gonzales-Black stated.

Other companies are experimenting with autonomy in various capacities.

- PwC is moving to a "guilt-free zone" work environment, urging associates to accommodate their team's personal needs, whether it's going to a yoga class every Tuesday or attending their kids' weekly soccer games. This also means for associates who travel, teams now assess whether everyone needs to be on-site with the client every week, or if the work can get done by alternating which team members travel.

- McKinsey employees are now allowed to take up to 10 weeks off between projects to pursue their personal interests. It's unpaid time but employees get to keep their benefits, and it's on top of regular paid vacation time. The firm also introduced the Pace Program to give employees more control over their career trajectory. This plan replaces the previous "up-or-out" model that meant people had to leave if they didn't advance at regular intervals.

- GE, once notorious for its rank-and-yank system, which mandated the bottom 10 percent of performers be fired, has moved away from numeric ratings. Its businesses are now experimenting with more frequent, qualitative, and even immediate feedback options as part of the company's switch to performance development. After a commissioned group of Millennials told GE what they wanted to see in company culture, the firm is trying to move from a command-and-control management model to a faster, simpler culture where individual teams have more autonomy to experiment and make decisions.

- Barr Engineering Co. has what they refer to as a "free-market structure" that allows employees to choose the projects they want to work on. Employees don't have bosses, per se. If they sign up as individual contributors on a project, they'll report to the manager of the chosen project. On other projects, they may serve as manager. When employees log long hours, they may choose to be paid for the overtime or take comp days.

- Pfizer sums up its company culture with two words: Own it. The company believes employees should be able to take ownership of their careers, allowing them the freedom to take risks and the support to confront systems and attitudes that aren't working.

## Knowledge and Talent

The rise of the Talent Economy indicates organizations are powered more by innovation and ideas than ever before, and knowledge and expertise have become as critical, and in some cases more, as other economic resources. That's why some people refer to the Talent Economy as the Knowledge Economy. This isn't new information. The economic shift was first identified in the 1990s, alongside the evolution of Google and other dot-com companies. Yet here we are 20 years later, and organizations are still struggling to transition.

Millennials have come of age during the Talent Economy; they have little to no memory of the Industrial Era and therefore no appreciation or understanding of processes and traditions and doing things the way they've always been done. This is a generation that has only known a world powered by knowledge: innovation, globalization, information, connectivity, and expertise. Anything else will seem foreign and irrelevant to them. They will struggle to comprehend why the bylaws can't be changed, why decisions can't be made on the fly, why they have to join a chapter to be part of an international association, and who the heck Robert is and why associations are still using his ridiculous Rules of Order.

Organizations rooted in the past will struggle to engage a generation progressing towards the future, which is why so many organizations are facing challenges in hiring, engaging, and retaining top talent. Since the 1960s, on-the-job training has been recognized as a contributing factor to organizational success. Learning and development have evolved considerably since then. Today, learning must address time and budget constraints, while at the same time being aware of the differing attitudes of the multi-generational workforce. Today, learning must take place at all phases of an employee's career, from entry-level to senior management.

From self-driving vehicles and semi-autonomous robots to intelligent algorithms and predictive analytics tools, machines are increasingly capable of performing a wide range of jobs that have long been human domains. A study by researchers at Oxford University posited that as many as 47 percent of all jobs in the United States are at risk of "computerization." And many respondents in a Pew Research Center study predicted that advances in robotics and computing applications will result in a net displacement of jobs over the coming decades, with potentially profound implications for both workers and society as a whole.

As automation looms, 63 percent of full- and part-time workers say they have taken steps in the past 12 months to upgrade their skills and knowledge. That is one of several key findings from a Pew Research Center survey conducted to understand people's motives for learning, both in professional and personal contexts. Here are some of the key themes that came out of Pew's study about learning, work, and a changing economy:

- The Great Recession led to soul-searching and skills re-evaluation. Many employees took stock of their skill set and employability after the economic collapse that began in 2007. As a result, employees (especially young professionals) want to continually pursue job-related training to maintain or improve their skills and increase their worth to employers.

- Competition is coming from every direction, including global- ization and new job entrants. Technology advances are only part of the story. People know jobs can be outsourced abroad or challenged by others in the local labor market.

- Sometimes people's rationale for job-related learning is defiance. There are those whose motivation for learning and upgrading their skills comes from proving their detractors wrong. This is especially apparent among young professionals who want to prove themselves and earn the respect of their employers.

- There is undeniable stress for many as they adjust to the new economy. Yet, most of the focus group participants positively embraced the idea of learning and found the process of learning pleasurable.

Companies in the United States spend an average $70 billion per year on training. Yet, many get low ROI on these programs, which is why the best companies are reshaping their learning strategies to focus on creating learning cultures and providing interactive learning environments. Consider the following:

- Google offers a program called Googler to Googler, which places employees in teaching roles. Googlers can teach courses on management and skills, such as public speaking. Other classes taught Googler to Googler—everything from kickboxing to parenting—are initiated and designed by employees. More than 2,000 Googlers have volunteered to teach classes, teaching about 55 percent of the company's official classes. The employee-to-employee teaching model promotes a culture of learning, encourages collaboration and community-building, and allows employees to bring their whole selves to work. In addition, learning is encouraged immediately. New employees are invited to pick three books out of a selection as a gift, and Google has several libraries on-site, too.

- Facebook is known for its innovative learning programs, focused on fostering collaborative relationships and continual learning throughout the organization. For example, the Engage Coaching Program provides new managers with one-on-one sessions with an executive coach to help them develop effective people management skills. The *FLiP* (Facebook Leadership in Practice) program delves into leadership best practices, case studies, team-building, and coaching circles where rising leaders receive feedback and coaching from their peers and Facebook executive team members. The *Managing Unconscious Bias* program trains employees to acknowledge bias in the workplace and build productive working relationships with co-workers.

Yelp executives actively mentor young employees. Pandora makes all its manager training available online and on-demand, and makes sure each session takes less than 15 minutes to complete. Learning is critical to competitiveness and it doesn't have to require elaborate resources or big budgets. Here are some tips that companies of any size can implement quickly to bring learning to their organizations:

- Promote in-house mentorship and coaching. Organize informal mentorship meet-ups, coaching circles, and peer-to-peer learning.

- Make on-line education an employee benefit. Companies like
  Udemy, Teachable, Lynda.com and Coursera all offer a variety of
  affordable subscriptions for employee on-line learning.

In a knowledge-driven economy, employers need to care far more
about learning and personal development than offering employees
free lunches, gym discounts, and ping pong.

## Sharing Economy

After defining ourselves for generations by possessions—cars, houses,
books, china patterns, stocks, boats, land, and jewelry—a dramatic
shift is under way. In the wake of a collapsed economy and a warming
planet, what matters to a growing number of young people is not so
much ownership as access.

More than a century ago consumption began to emerge as a driving
force and curator in American life. By the time the 1950s rolled around
(when Boomers were being born) families started moving to the
suburbs, accumulated possessions like new appliances, bigger cars,
and fancier houses, and tried to keep up with The Jones'.

Then businesses began rolling out new versions of products that
were somehow always better, faster, and smarter than the ones that
had come before. The psychological effects were powerful, and they're
still with us today—as anybody who has seen, or stood in, the lines
outside of an Apple store before the release of a new iPhone can
attest.

After a century of working even harder to own more, Millennials
seem to be stopping that ingrained societal cycle and changing the
concept of ownership. They are open to the idea of sharing more and
owning less.

It's no coincidence that Facebook has a "Share" button. Millennials
love sharing information via social media, but the Sharing Economy
moves way beyond technology. For example, Millennials are the
primary user of Zipcar, the world's largest car sharing company.

Airbnb is another prominent example of the Sharing Economy. Dubbed the world's largest community hospitality company, Airbnb is a website for people to list and rent out lodging, including apartments, castles, boats, manors, tree houses, tipis, igloos, private islands, and other properties. The company is currently valued at $30 billion.

Some of this sharing, of course, is a result of the economic downturn during the late 2000s. But that's not the whole story. EBay and Craigslist both launched in 1995, allowed people to buy and sell goods from one another. So it's not just an outcome of the recession. There's been a shift in mindset as well, and Millennials were born and raised amidst this new sharing era.

### Uber Arrives

The main take-away for every organization here is to never assume that your company is exempt from any change. Without a doubt, the car rental and taxi industry assumed people will always need transportation and the industries got a little too comfortable with that reality.

Today, Uber's ride-sharing service, barely eight years old, is valued at more than $68 billion. Whereas Enterprise, founded in 1957 and the largest car rental company, has a market value of less than $15 billion. Uber, Lyft and other app-enabled, sharing economy companies have disrupted the car rental business and traditional taxi business in a major way.

But when you consider the car rental process had remained largely the same for 60 years, sooner or later disruption was likely. Most of us have experienced the byzantine process of picking up a rental car, which at an airport often involves waiting for a bus, then standing in line at the rental car counter, dragging luggage through a parking lot, and painfully slow customer service. It's hard to deny that simply tapping your smartphone and waiting curbside for Uber is far easier, and in many cases, more cost efficient.

Industry leaders Avis, Enterprise, and Hertz claim to understand the looming challenge. Each has taken steps to blunt the competition—mostly riding on the "coattails" of the sharing economy pioneers. Avis, for example, is expanding its Zipcar-sharing service that enables members to pick up a car from designated parking spaces in certain downtown areas and college campuses and drop them off just as easily. Hertz signed an agreement to provide older cars to Uber and Lyft drivers who might not have cars of their own. Enterprise has a similar agreement with Uber. There also are efforts to have rental cars delivered to drivers as a way of eliminating lines.

But overall the industry has been slow to embrace the massive changes that are needed to compete in the new era where digital

## Trends Chart

Going forward, the only way your organization will remain relevant is if you are aware of the marketplace trends and technology breakthroughs. Futurists refer to this as environmental scanning. Identify trends affecting your organization and write them down in the Trends Chart.

From here, you can facilitate discussions with stakeholders on the implications of the trends, such as possible risks and opportunities, and identify what other trends are happening in conjunction.

By understanding trends your organization can design an aspirational future not based upon legacy thinking, but one that is fully aware of changing dynamics and designed to be responsive and relevant.

| Trend | Causes | Potential Impact | Anticipated Evolution |
|-------|--------|------------------|-----------------------|
|       |        |                  |                       |
|       |        |                  |                       |
|       |        |                  |                       |
|       |        |                  |                       |
|       |        |                  |                       |

technology rules. At this point, car rental companies are so late in recognizing the need for change and will struggle to regain their lead against ride-sharing companies.

Is there a lesson here? Yes. It's "stay future-focused." Listen to the customer, pay attention to market trends, never stop innovating, and never ever assume your organization is unrivaled.

## Impact Economy

To Millennials, the world is filled with injustice and need, but government isn't the solution. They may be slightly less radical than their Baby Boomer parents, whose demonstrations for civil rights, women's equality, and protests against the Vietnam War became flashpoints for their times. Still, the apple didn't fall far from the tree. Millennials want to change the world, and they are much more aware of the world because of their access to technology.

This generation came of age during the Iraq War and the war in Afghanistan and has observed several tragedies close to home, such as the 9/11 terrorist attacks, global warming, Amber Alerts, suicides, school shootings, and Hurricane Katrina. This is a generation that's concerned about global warming, broadly supports equality for the LGBT community, has no qualms about interracial marriage, and is much more diverse and civic-minded than other generations.

Put all these influences together—a world rocked by change, faced daily with new information and threats to survival, and a stalled government—and you get a generation that believes the only way to improve the situation is by innovation and taking matters into their own hands.

That's why Millennials are more likely to be social entrepreneurs working for social enterprises, meaning they prefer to work outside government to create innovative and measurably successful solutions to the nation's problems. The terms "social enterprise" and "social entrepreneur" means this generation engages in collaborative problem solving (social) and takes the initiative to make a positive change (entrepreneurship) or works for a company that seeks to make positive social change (enterprise).

When interviewed about *Fortune*'s Change the World List, featuring 50 companies which are doing well by doing good, Nicholas Varchaver, Assistant Managing Editor, cautioned: "It's not a list of companies and their charity." Rather, organizations that are excelling in this area have made social responsibility "core to their business as opposed to a little side project."

Glaxo SmithKline (GSK), a pharmaceutical company, topped the 2016 list for its decision to no longer file drug patents in the lowest-income regions of the world, thus lowering prices and providing more access to medication. GSK reinvests 20 percent of any profits it makes in the least developed countries into training health workers and building medical infrastructure. For instance, through a partnership with the non-governmental organization Save the Children, the drugmaker has trained locals to properly administer vaccinations and screen for conditions like malnutrition.

According to *Fortune*'s report, GSK leaders said the approach builds goodwill and a strong market presence around the globe. Leaders credit the company's continued success to not just thinking about the next year or two, but what GSK needs to do to be successful in the next several decades. (By the way, the company's roots extend back to 1715.)

Nike was listed among the top 10 on *Fortune*'s 2016 Change the World list. According to the report, Mark Parker, CEO, likes to ask his team a single question: "Can we double our business, while halving our environmental impact?" The world's largest athletic gear company first kicked off a recycled shoe program back in 1990 and has hit a steady sustainability stride ever since. About 71 percent of Nike's footwear and apparel uses Nike Grind, which is made of recycled polyester and other materials. Engineers reduced waste by 60 percent for the Flyknit shoe line, saving nearly 2 million pounds of fabric-scrap waste since 2012. It's these types of attitudes that are leading in the Talent Economy.

According to the eighth annual Deloitte Volunteer IMPACT Survey, 70 percent of Millennials strongly favor companies committed to the community. In fact, Millennials who frequently participate in workplace volunteer activities are twice as likely to rate their workforce culture as very positive, 19 percent more likely to feel proud to work for their company, and 19 percent more likely to feel very loyal toward their company. In other words, they are more likely to be engaged employees.

Consider Patagonia, whose mission statement highlights the company's commitment toward the environment: Build the best product, cause no unnecessary harm, use business to inspire and implement solutions to the environmental crisis. Patagonia's mission is pretty clear, and the company also cites its reason for being:

> For us at Patagonia, a love of wild and beautiful places demands participation in the fight to save them, and to help reverse the steep decline in the overall environmental health of our planet. We donate our time, services and at least 1 percent of our sales to hundreds of grassroots environmental groups all over the world who work to help reverse the tide.

The company hasn't wavered from its core values since it was founded in 1973. In 2016, Patagonia's employee turnover was referred to as "freakishly low" by *Fortune* magazine. Patagonia has 2,000 employees. In a survey of 550 employees, 97 percent said they feel good about the ways Patagonia contributes to the community.

Service to others and service to the team are equally important to Millennials. Patagonia has an on-site child care center that is run by teachers, some of whom are bilingual and trained in child development. Learning takes place outdoors as much as in. Parents often eat lunch with their children, take them to the farmer's market, or pick vegetables with them. Patagonia buses school-aged kids back to the company's headquarters, allowing parents to connect with them after school over chocolate milk.

Patagonia's child care program was not put in place to fight the war for talent, or because its executives wanted to fix the leaky pipeline of women leaving before reaching senior management levels. Rather, the company's founders saw a need and wanted to fulfill it. They wanted to support their friends and family as they worked and responded to what their talent needed. Amazingly, 100 percent of the women who have had children at Patagonia over the past five years have returned to work, significantly higher than the 79 percent average in the United States.

Millennials want more from their employer than just a paycheck, they want a sense of pride and to feel the company's values match their own.

## Digital Economy

Generation Y is the first generation to have never known life without technology. We all know this to be true, but do we really comprehend what that means? It means this generation prefers to never be more than literally a few feet away from a technology device. It means this generation values access to technology more than dating. It means this generation considers access to technology a basic need, valuing it as much as freedom and oxygen on basic needs assessments. Crazy as it may sound, Millennials can't fathom a life without technology because they've never known life without it.

As Digital Natives, Millennials are more reliant on technology, more comfortable using technology, and tend to be among the first to try new technologies. Networked their entire lives, Millennials love being part of the global conversation that social media affords and accessing information via apps.

## Management by App

Keeping the digital shift top of mind, General Electric recently introduced an app designated for employee feedback. For decades, General Electric (GE) practiced a rigid system frequently called "rank and yank," which boiled the employees' performance down to a number on which they were judged and ranked against their peers. The bottom 10 percent of underperformers were then fired. At the time, this intense approach made sense, as GE faced extraordinary competition and cost-cutting and quality control were imperative.

Now, GE is opting for a less regimented system via an app. This move likely represents the beginning of the end for the annual review practice that has been at the heart of how organizations managed people for decades. Over time, the process had become more ritual than moving the company upwards and forwards, which was a sign it was time to let it go. Let's face it. There are few companies in America that have General Electric's legacy. Founded by none other than the great inventor Thomas Edison, it's well into its second century of existence.

But the world doesn't run on an annual cycle anymore and the workforce has changed. Millennials are used to getting feedback which is more frequent, faster, and mobile-enabled. The annual review, which tends to look in the rearview mirror, simply does not suit today's future-facing workforce.

The new app, PD@GE (Performance Development at GE), was built by a team of GE's software engineers. Each employee has a series of goals, referred to as priorities, and managers are expected to have frequent discussions, called touchpoints, on progress toward those goals noting what was discussed, committed to, and resolved. The app can provide typed summaries, photographs, and voice recordings.

Employees can give or request feedback at any point through a feature called Insights, which isn't limited to their immediate manager or even their division. This allows for timely feedback and immediate change and encourages managers to engage as "coaches" with their team. The app forces users to categorize feedback in one of two forms: to continue doing something or to consider changing something. Managers will still be expected to have an annual summary conversation with employees every December to look back at the year and set goals.

### Engagement by Emoji

Is it possible to pinpoint precisely who is on the verge of quitting? Yes. Using emojis? Yes.

In 2013, Sears launched a platform in-house for gathering data on morale from hourly workers. Each day, when employees punched out at the end of their shifts, workers were asked, "How's your mood?" Employees were asked to tap an emoji—happy face, mad, blah, neutral, or whichever reflected their state of mind at that moment. However, the symbol people tapped mattered far less than whether they bothered to choose any at all.

HR managers quickly realized that if a store showed a significant drop in employees picking an emoji, that store had a big attrition problem 30 to 60 days later. The same pattern showed up among salaried employees.

"It was remarkably accurate," stated Dean Carter, a former HR executive for Sears in *Fortune*. "What you want to watch out for is a change in participation. If someone has been weighing in often, or regularly, and then suddenly stops, that's when you might have a problem."

Now as head of HR and Shared Services at Patagonia, Carter has called on an employee-engagement software provider to set up a system similar to what he'd been using at Sears. Holding on to key

talent means companies need to capture the voice of the employee—
in real time, and not just once a year.

## Employee Engagement. Now.

Not many people have an opportunity to meet and work with both
a United States president and Richard Branson, the billionaire
entrepreneur who runs more than 60 businesses. But Trista Harris,
president of the Minnesota Council on Foundations, had the
opportunity to meet both within the course of a couple years.

Harris, who knew she wanted to work with nonprofits since the
age of 8, has been studying futurism and how to use it to solve social
problems. Her opportunity to attend two future-focused events,
South by South Lawn at the White House, and a futurist conference
hosted by Branson on Necker Island, furthered her concerns about
the widespread lack of planning occurring throughout organizations
worldwide.

"I think there are a lot of changes that are happening in the
world that we're just not talking about in the nonprofit sector, and
nonprofits should really be at the forefront of these conversations."
She rattled off a list of developments on the immediate horizon:
artificial intelligence, robotics, DNA technology which can identify if
you have stage 0 cancer, self-driving cars, the move toward working
fewer hours or part-time, universal basic incomes, and the need to
revamp higher education due to its expense and inability to equip the
workforce with skillsets needed for today's jobs.

Just one of these changes has the potential to make a huge
difference in how our communities operate. Considering all of them
at once has made it difficult for leaders to navigate and cope, Harris
said. "When you go through such a period of transition, people are
not made for this pace of change. They get crabby, they start blaming
each other," she said. Others avoid the subject altogether. "I think
the leaders of many organizations are saying: 'I have no idea what

you're talking about. It's not part of the conversations we're having in this sector.' That needs to change." Harris said it's imperative that all organizations ask: How do we rebuild society around what we're going to be next, rather than what we used to be.

She also urged for the inclusion of younger generations, noting that the White House's South by South Lawn event had children as young as 12 years old present, who were developing new medical technologies, drones, and other game-changing products and services.

"The workforce is changing and the expectations of our workforce are changing. Hopefully we understand that the diversity of perspective and new ways of doing work is critical as our organizations transition," she said.

Based on six years of research, Harris developed a simple model to help organizations successfully progress toward future-focused change initiatives. The model is Stop, Look, and Go. She explained:

- *Stop* is a reminder to stop loving the problem. Stop feeling like the future is something that just happens to you, rather than what you create with your work.

- *Look* is a reminder to pay attention to trends. "There's a million signals of what the future is going to look like, and we need to spend a lot of time paying attention to those things. I'd love to see a leader spend 5 percent of their time on research and development—paying attention to what's coming next, and what it means for your organization."

- *Go* is a reminder to try new things and to not be afraid to fail. "Build experiments within your organization so that you can figure out what a trend might mean for the work that you're doing. Then share what you've learned with your peers, even if it doesn't work. That's the part that people don't like to do. Share your successes, but also share the parts that are really difficult or didn't work, so somebody else doesn't bump their head in the same spot. All this work is too big to do alone, so we need to figure out how to do it together."

Harris is right. Change isn't an option, and we're all in this boat together. While Millennials are the first generation to come of age in the Post-Industrial era—and their values, needs, wants, interests and expectations have been shaped by these micro-economies that compose the Talent Economy—their arrival is only the tip of the iceberg. There are much bigger changes on the horizon.

## Dedicated to the Future

Bob Moritz was willing to admit that although PwC hired 8,000 young professionals each year, the company assumed too much, didn't realize the magnitude of change happening under their very noses, and didn't take the time to understand the changing needs of the Millennial workforce. It wasn't until the company invested in an employee survey that PwC realized they were on the wrong path. And they set out to change course.

"When I was coming up, we knew what we were doing, but we didn't ask why we did it," he wrote. Moritz goes on to explain that PwC had continued to assume that there would always be employees who accepted the notion of making partner "as the reward and justification for years of long hours" in service to clients. But PwC's study revealed that the allure of someday becoming partner, and even the prospect of substantial future compensation, wasn't enough to engage Millennials.

Rather, the Millennial workforce wanted job flexibility in the here and now, along with opportunities for training and mobility and better and more frequent feedback and rewards. PwC's leaders realized they "had to respond to this research in a radical way," Moritz wrote. So PwC turned its traditional human-capital approach on its head. Millennials asked to have more input on important issues. PwC responded by:

- Being more intentional about engaging and informing all employees;

- Asking employees for ideas on how to invest in human capital and what the firm's next $100 million idea should be (70 percent of the organization took part in the ideation process); and

- Expanding choice in many areas—including bonuses. Employees may receive their rewards as cash, gift cards, product packages, or even matched charitable contributions.

Millennials asked for more appreciation. PwC responded by:

- Implementing several non-monetary rewards for staying with the firm, such as leadership training retreats or a four-week sabbatical during which they can pursue an interest, travel, volunteer, or stay at home with the family.

Millenials asked managers to change their attitudes toward them. PwC responded by:

- Introducing education to address stereotypes and assumptions, and helping Boomers understand that Millennials are committed to the success of the firm, but not prepared to sacrifice their health and well-being for it.

Millennials asked for more flexibility. PwC responded by:

- Reinforcing the value of work-life flexibility for managers, asking them how team members will be enabled to shift work hours or work remotely before being promoted to a managerial role;

- Rewarding the managers who model flexible behavior in their compensation;

- Creating a contest to solicit ideas for a flexibility plan for PwC's busy season (more than half the firm's employees participated);

- Explaining to clients up front that PwC will provide a *team* that's going to be there 24/7—not an individual; and

- Overstaffing teams so that no one person has to be unduly burdened for the sake of a deal.

Moritz said these changes experienced some push-back. "It's not uncommon for our longer-term partners and staff to believe that working hard is, or should be, a badge of honor," he said.

Likewise, he noted that "a greater emphasis on nontraditional career models sometimes gives our clients pause."

Nevertheless, PwC learned the benefits of sticking to its people commitments. Over the past decade turnover has decreased by about three percentage points—while employee engagement has increased by three percentage points.

In the end, Moritz realized that Millennials are just as committed to their units and to the firm as previous generations. Their definition of commitment has changed, as this generation refuses to sacrifice their health or personal lives for their jobs. But their devotion to the missions of the client and the firm have not wavered. And clearly, PwC's devotion to its talent has not wavered, either.

**CHAPTER SUMMARY**

Generation Y (1982–1995), also known as Millennials, came of age during a time of economic recession, digital innovation, and political revolution. In fact, their arrival was accompanied by five currents of change that are so powerful they have been referred to as mini-economies within the Talent Economy. The Sharing, Gig, Knowledge, Experience, and Impact economies are spurring unprecedented social, economic, and political change on a global scale.

Not surprising, these economies have shaped the opinions, values, and behaviors of this generation in radical ways—which will undoubtedly shape *every* generation's opinions, values, and behaviors and have already begun to do so. It's the Trickle-Up Effect. Sooner or later, the youngest generation influences the older generations, and this is how widespread change often occurs.

There is much to learn from this generation and much potential that has yet to be tapped.

**QUESTIONS TO CONSIDER**

1. What are the trends affecting your industry and organization?

2. On a scale of 1–5 (1 being awful and 5 being awesome) how would you rank your organization's current proficiency at the following?

   \_\_\_\_ Learning about the trends and the interests of the young people likely to influence your organization's future.

   \_\_\_\_ Accepting and acting upon the trends and the values, needs, and interests of the young people likely to influence your organization's future.

   \_\_\_\_ Thinking about and planning for a desired future.

   \_\_\_\_ Being a valuable resource to others by helping stakeholders (board, volunteers, members, or clients) prepare for the future.

3. If young professionals, between the ages of 28 and 35, were put in charge of your organization, what would they do differently? (If you're uncertain, ask some young people this question.) What would happen if your organization did these same things now?

4. If your organization refuses to change and avoids planning for the future, what might be the long-term consequences?

*The previous chapters addressed the need for a people first and future-focused strategy. The next step is teamwork. Employee engagement is achieved when people care about the organization and the people working for it, which is why teamwork is important.*

*"Great things are never done by one person.*
*They're done by a team of people."*

STEVE JOBS

· · · · · · · · · · · · · · · · · · · · · · · · · · · ·

## CHAPTER 6

# Collaborate

When HealthCare.gov debuted on October 1, 2013, the site crashed so often that of the millions who came to the site, virtually no one was able to complete an application. The failure threatened not only the controversial Affordable Care Act but the legacy of President's Obama's administration.

Todd Park was among those asked to help rescue the endeavor. The Chief Technology Officer of the United States had not been involved in creating the site, but as the designated fixer he realized that he would need outsiders, engineers schooled in a different style of computing than those who botched the project. Before his stint in government, Park had started two medical IT companies, and it was that experience, not policy or politics, that he called upon. Park recruited a half-dozen engineers from various tech companies. This small team, working around the clock in Maryland, fixed the site in seven hectic weeks.

Not only did the effort "save the president's baby," as one former White House staffer put it, it crystallized within the administration the impact that just a handful of deeply talented techies could have on our government's functionality. And it prompted President Obama,

Park, and their colleagues to wonder: Could an infusion of West Coast tech talent become permanent? What might that achieve?

So Park began recruiting an elite digital corps, a startup team built mainly from the ranks of top private-sector companies, and embedded them within the U.S. government. The President personally helped Park and his team hire talent and implement their ideas across a host of government agencies. Their purpose was to remake the digital systems by which government operates—not exactly a small order or quick fix.

President Obama envisioned building a pipeline of tech talent in Washington that would implement the kind of efficiency and agility that define Silicon Valley's largest technology companies into government agencies. Simply by upgrading the government's technology and websites of organizations like the Veterans Administration, users could access crucial services that save time, money—even lives.

## The Collaboration Generation

Remember bound volumes of reports in the company library? Secretaries who took the boss' dictation? Executives who shut their office doors and emerged with full blown strategies for business?

Depending on where you are in your career, these may be real but ancient history. For younger generations, this probably sounds like something straight out of *Mad Men* or an old movie, both a laughable and unfathomable past.

As a Gen Xer, I feel as though I had a front row seat to the evolution from Industrial Era to Talent Economy. From the time I was quite young, I spent quite a lot of time at work with my Dad. Those experiences left a lasting impression on me.

This was the era of suits and stockings, respect, hierarchy, and formalities. As the president of the bank, the employees always addressed my Dad as "Mr. Ruble." If I wanted to call him during the week, the conversation had to be brief. Personal phone calls at work were frowned upon. On Saturdays, the bank was closed, but my Dad often went into work anyway. I remember accompanying him when I was quite young, walking among the empty desks, imagining I was performing for an audience or running a company, or drawing pictures in his office.

My dad retired 12 years ago—before smart phones and tablets, Wi-Fi, cloud computing, and all other things flexible, mobile, and virtual. He doesn't understand why people are sitting in Starbucks having meetings, talking on their phones, and discussing business in such a casual, open format. When he grouses about this, I realize how much has changed in recent years. Even though the Talent Economy began in 1996, society didn't fully begin to embrace it until several years later—right around the time my dad retired.

Exclusivity, hierarchy, and solitude have since been replaced by radically different ways of collaborative working. People increasingly work in places other than their offices (much to my father's dismay) and on teams that draw expertise from virtually anywhere in the world. They access applications, data, and subject matter experts, and employ whatever end-user device is right for the job to improve productivity, while enhancing the work experience for themselves and their employees.

Collaboration is often seen as an activity that involves team members working on a project together. True collaboration isn't limited to doing one project or something that's done every once in a while; it is a strategy which maximizes individual contribution while leveraging the collective intelligence of everyone involved.

In a truly collaborative environment, everyone has a voice (always) and contributes (continually). When people understand how their contributions fit into the organization's strategy, it gives them purpose. With that purpose comes belief and trust in the organization, its leaders, and co-workers. Purpose and belief translate into higher levels of employee engagement.

At the most basic level, people want to feel a sense of belonging. For this reason, collaboration should take center stage in every organization because, more than anything else, it creates an environment in which employees feel like they belong. In collaboration, employees feel empowered, take ownership, build relationships, and feel respected, valuable, and important. Collaboration increases employee energy, creativity, and productivity, which generally leads to less stressed, happier, and more engaged workers.

As many organizations can attest, however, collaboration is difficult to sustain. After all, collaboration hasn't been the norm in the workforce. Prior generations were raised to be self-sufficient, working in organizations dictated by hierarchies and silos, relying almost exclusively on individual contributions and knowledge. Therefore, it's proven quite challenging to switch over to a hyper-connected, on-demand, work-anywhere-anytime workforce in which ideas—and therefore collaboration—are now the competitive advantage.

The following chart cites just a few of the ways you can determine whether your organization is poised for collaboration and working in the Talent Economy, or stuck in the past.

| Industrial Era | Talent Economy |
|---|---|
| Certain employees or departments bring value to the company and are empowered to introduce new ideas | Everyone has a voice and is encouraged to introduce new ideas; value is created alongside clients, vendors, alumni |
| Ideas come from within, usually from those employees with the most experience or knowledge | Ideas come from inside or outside the organization, transcending geographic borders, job descriptions, and age ranges |
| Value is based on an employee's skills and knowledge | Value is based on an employee's ability to work with others |
| Information is owned and protected | Information is shared |
| Work is largely document-focused, connecting systems and data | Work is largely people-focused, connecting people, ideas, and knowledge |
| Individuals or small groups work to solve problems and innovate | Large groups work to solve problems and innovate |
| The organization's structure is defined and roles are specialized | The organization's structure and workforce roles are constantly emerging |

The organization that does not move toward collaboration may lose significant business advantages, critical talent, and the ability to attract talented employees from the emerging workforce. It may reduce the speed and scope of its ability to innovate. It may lose credibility with clients. It may lose business to others with greater innovation. It may be unable to capture growth in new market segments. It almost certainly will lose efficiencies, and may even increase its cost of doing business. The organization that fails to collaborate will fail to innovate. So how do we move an organization towards collaboration?

## Kickstarting Collaboration

Most organizations assert they want to be innovative and collaborative, but they approach these concepts as separate efforts or skill
sets. Research at the University of Tennessee has found innovation
and collaboration are not mutually exclusive. They build upon each
other. Innovation naturally happens through and exists within collaboration. And the best organizations harness innovation from their
employees and outsiders—especially those from younger generations.

When we think of great innovations, we might instinctively think
of them as the product of a sudden brainstorm from an individual. It's
the cartoon character with a lightbulb suddenly appearing over his
head. However, innovation is often produced over time with a lot of
collective sweat equity by many people.

This is likely why some organizations are struggling to innovate,
while others have become renowned for innovation. In the absence
of collaboration, holding steadfast to hierarchy and silos, innovation
is difficult—if not impossible—to achieve. And the longer those
hierarchies and silos stay in place, the more laggard these organizations become. (If this is the case, you will need to go back to the
previous steps outlined in this book, to revamp your organization's
leadership and employee engagement strategies.)

If your organization is ready for collaboration, there's much to learn
from the concepts of hackathons, accelerators, and incubators, all
designed to systematically build teamwork, belonging, collaboration,
and innovation into their operations.

### Hackathon

Hackathons are core to Facebook's culture, the mission being to
"move fast and break things." The company regularly designates time
for hackathons, and even organizes special hackathon events.

- Camp Hackathon took place across three days and two nights,
  which meant employees literally set up camp (yes, with tents)

at the Menlo Park campus. Full-time employees and interns worked together to innovate. The only rule: You couldn't work on anything that's part of your day-to-day job.

• Family Hackathons draw in over 700 guests who attend to "hack" with their children, nieces, and nephews, on projects designed to develop and support computer science, math, and building skills.

A hackathon is essentially a means for creative, collaborative problem solving. For example, at the 2015 Facebook Global Hackathon, a Carnegie Mellon University student team won the $10,000 grand prize by creating a news-focused digital product. Within 24 hours, the team developed Onreel.news, a website designed to let users track developing stories around the world in real-time through videos taken by eyewitnesses.

Hackathons were originally designed to be a sprint-like event in which computer programmers, graphic designers, interface designers, project managers, and others collaborate intensively on innovation. However, the hackathon concept has morphed into a business strategy.

Likeable Local, a social media company started hosting hackathons for their team to focus on improving the business. Of their 40 employees, only six are developers. The rest of the team is comprised of sales, marketing, customer service, and creative professionals. By hosting three "hack mornings" in a single quarter, and challenging the whole company to engage, the firm reported improved collaboration, morale, productivity. "There's nothing like exploring a new project for hours together, uninterrupted to bond teammates with one another. Team morale has been higher than ever before, thanks to these hackathons," CEO Dave Kerpen wrote in a guest post for *Inc.*

Likeable Local's team dedicated two hours to each hackathon, which Kerpen said didn't seem like much time, yet the team managed to build programs, email templates, campaigns, and many other projects during those condensed periods of time.

"Working hard, working fast, working tirelessly, working intensely, and working with your team. What entrepreneur or leader wouldn't want their employees to embrace these values?," Kerpen wrote. "While it's difficult if not impossible to maintain the hackathon pace and drive during most workdays, it's amazing for everyone to see how much can actually get done when there are no meetings, no phone calls, and no interruptions—just people working together towards a common goal."

## Accelerator

Accelerators were created to start up companies through education, mentorship, and financing. Learning-by-doing is vital to the process of scaling start-up ventures, and the point of accelerators is to accelerate that process, compressing years' worth of learning into a period of a few months.

Start-ups are usually characterized by an extremely inspirational, driven atmosphere. By involving a company's employees in accelerators with start-ups, and appointing them as mentors or organizing events such as innovation workshops or pitch nights, elements of the start-up atmosphere transfers into the company culture which inspires employees in terms of innovation and collaboration.

For example, the Volkswagen Group of America Electronics Research Laboratory (ERL) launched a tech start-up accelerator program to bring innovation in-house. Chosen start-ups participate in a three-month program, featuring access to investors, corporations, and mentors plus tech events, educational seminars, and office space. On the flipside, Volkswagen's team gets the opportunity to collaborate with some of the brightest minds in technology to help define the future direction of automobiles.

In brief, corporations running accelerators get to observe start-up teams and trends in action, and often identify new opportunities or areas in which the business may be at risk for disruption. Finding ways for your organization to mimic this experience is important.

Here are examples of two different accelerator-themed programs:

- Ford Motor Co.'s Thirty Under 30 is a yearlong course which represents Ford's ongoing initiative to develop young employee leaders who also serve their communities. Annually, 30 employees, all under the age of 30, take time away from their jobs as Ford engineers, financial, marketing, and IT professionals to learn what it takes to run a charity, and develop strategies for the nonprofits to connect with younger generations of donors and volunteers. As a result, Ford's employees gain valuable skills, and both Ford and the participating charitable organizations have the opportunity to learn from one another.

- The Brooklyn Fashion + Design Accelerator (BF+DA), the "hub for ethical fashion and design," was established to provide designers with the resources they need to transform their ideas into successful businesses. In addition to having 21,000 square feet of production and work space, members receive access to mentoring, small-run apparel production, digital fabrication services, showroom space, materials sourcing, and links to existing NYC manufacturers. BF+DA's residency program provides a year of mentorship on business development and expert counseling on sustainable strategies, production, materiality, and wearable technology. In addition, BF+DA curates educational programs and events to deliver programming on business-building strategies and design tools and techniques.

In an accelerator, relationships are mutually beneficial. There's much to be learned and gained in an accelerator. Collaborations are forged, valuable skills and knowledge are shared, and this ultimately leads to innovation and catapults individuals and entities to greater success.

## Incubator

While accelerators tend to focus on high growth during a short-term project, incubators take a long-term approach with mentorship or relationship-building periods often lasting more than a year and a half.

In my opinion, every organization should be thinking of themselves as incubators. The Talent Economy is marked by a never-ending cycle of change and disruption, which means training and innovation also need to continue without end, for young professionals and executives alike.

Here again, incubators were originally designed to house start-up companies and equip them with the guidance, skills, and support they needed to develop and grow. Since then, there are many variations on the incubator theme appearing in all types of organizations for all types of purposes.

- Massachusetts Biomedical Initiatives helps launch biomedical companies and create jobs within the biotechnology, medical device, informatics, and biomanufacturing industries. This incubator relies on collaboration to further the industry, forging strategic partnerships with an array of local colleges and universities to provide access to equipment, talent, business support, and access to private, secured labs. Since its founding in 1985, the incubator has launched 150 companies and created over 2,500 jobs.

- Seattle is home to the Women's Business Incubator, a co-working, co-play space for entrepreneurs. The incubator features an on-site preschool and co-working office space. Members also have access to leadership training circles, micro-loans and financing, mentoring, training, and business services.

- Time Inc. is facing challenges as it tries to transition to the digital age, and decided to use the incubator concept to foster an internal think tank comprised of Millennial employees. New Media Upstarts is comprised of 600 Millennial employees, providing guidance on what Time Inc. should be doing to engage Millennials as consumers and how to help young professionals be more effective in their jobs. In turn, team members from New Media Upstarts receive mentoring and access to executives, and play an active role in the company. Team members have hosted company-wide events and their input led to a new benefits option that lets employees lower their health-care costs by taking spin classes and wearing Fitbits. Time Inc. reports that not a week goes by that the Millennials aren't engaged in some aspect of running or influencing the business.

The future will likely be won by those who don't wait for light-bulb moments from a single genius, but rather develop highly collaborative win-win relationships that leverage the collective power of many. Steve Jobs, co-founder and former CEO of Apple, referred to this as the development of grassroots intelligence networks.

## Grassroots Intelligence Networks

In his book, *The Steve Jobs Way: iLeadership for a New Generation,* author Jay Elliot, former Senior Vice President of Apple and a close colleague of Steve Jobs, wrote about Jobs' approach within Apple. Elliot explained that under Jobs' leadership, Apple fostered an entrepreneurial environment, always challenging and encouraging employees to share their ideas and creativity in alignment with Apple's vision. He wrote:

Through encouraging employees and their ideas, you get a grassroots intelligence network. Employees bring in new things in the market and talk about them, discuss their advantages and shortcoming, test them, play with them, and then wonder, What can we do that's a generation better?

In contrast to Apple's approach, Elliot writes that in traditional companies, people are so focused on productivity and profits that they don't have time to look at things from a radically different perspective. As a result, there isn't much cross-pollination, because too many companies keep a "playpen" for the really bright people, separating them from the rest of the organization. This limits the potential of the employees and the entire organization.

Which category does your organization fall into: one that fosters grassroots intelligence or one that monitors intelligence via a playpen? I've seen evidence of playpens in several organizations.

- It's the executive team, which meets behind closed doors and has their own retreats, but rarely interacts with the rest of the staff.

- It's the board of directors, wielding decision-making power over an organization, yet spending little to no time within the organization itself.

- It's an executive's decision to not allow a young employee attend a conference, for fear a competing company will meet the employee and try to hire him away.

- It's the creation of young professionals' groups in membership associations. The association doesn't want to give the young professionals any influence yet, so they create a "playpen" where younger members can congregate and have their own board and organize their own events.

Not surprising, these tend to be the organizations grappling with turnover, negative cultures, and a lack of innovation. Regimentation isn't beneficial, in fact it's quite detrimental to an organization, and its era has long since come to an end.

In the Industrial Era, playpens supported a workforce organized by silos and driven by hierarchy. In the Talent Economy, playpens prohibit talent generation and must be eliminated from the workforce to allow for cognitive diversity and collaboration.

## Cognitive Diversity

I previously sat on a board of directors for a national membership association, and I vividly recall the struggle for that board to get anything done. Board meetings were fraught with debates, tension, and inefficiency, and they were unproductive. Thinking back on the experience, I believe part of the challenge was that the board was comprised of people who largely thought and processed information in the exact same way. We all came from similar professional experiences and backgrounds, and most board members fell within about a 10-year age range of one another. It was a homogenous group. Too homogenous.

I've since observed many other organizations with a similar power structure and similar challenge. Everyone is about the same age, the same gender or race, and from the same profession. Is it any wonder then why they would use the word "stuck" to describe their organizations?

A study by Nielsen discovered that larger teams, comprised of a variety of skillsets, generate better ideas. Nielsen asked teams of various sizes to develop pre-market concepts that were tested with consumers. Teams of six or more people generated concepts that performed 58 percent better than the concepts developed by individuals, and teams of two people performed only 16 percent better than the individuals.

Nielsen's research also proved that teams comprised of different functional roles (in this case marketing, consumer insights, sales, research, and development) delivered better concepts. Teams with representatives from four or more functions generated concepts that performed 46 percent better than the teams with fewer functional roles represented. In other words, the more cognitive diversity a team has, the more innovative it is.

Geil Browning is a brain researcher and the founder and CEO of Emergenetics International, a psychometric research company, which has landed on the Inc. 5000 List of Fastest Growing Companies the past six years in a row.

Browning has published articles on collaboration, explaining that collaboration is fueled by cognitive diversity, which is the practice of bringing different thinking styles into an organization. In their psychometric studies, Emergenetics analyzes four thinking attributes, named and color-coded as follows:

- The analytical brain (blue) enjoys math and science, tends to be objective and facts-driven, and is a logical problem solver. It enjoys all aspects of analysis: assessing strengths and weaknesses, weighing pros and cons, prioritizing, segmenting. It seeks to find the meaning behind the data.

- The structural brain (green) thinks practically. True to its name, it craves structure: plans, guidelines, processes, procedures, rules. The green brain tends to be predictable, trusting the tried and true and cautious of the new and different.

- The social brain (red) is intuitive about people. It's socially aware and likes caring for others. It's where our empathy lies. The red brain favors a humanistic management approach with a leadership style that's consultative, facilitating discussion and interaction.

- The conceptual brain (yellow) is the seat of our imagination. It is intuitive about ideas, associated with creativity, and seeking the new and different. The yellow brain has a sense of adventure and enjoys the unusual. It's strategic and visionary in its approach.

Every Emergenetics employee takes the personality profile and the results are displayed on the walls of the Emergenetics office.

"This helps create an atmosphere of openness. Each person can understand how conversations are likely to go with other staffers— and who to tap for a different way of thinking or action," Browning wrote in an article about the company's approach to collaboration.

The aggregate profile of the Emergenetics team is almost perfectly balanced between analytical, conceptual, social, and structural thinking preferences. This is all by design. Understanding the importance of cognitive diversity, Browning wanted a team of diverse thinkers and behavior types. "If you've got a lot of one type of thinking or behavior, seek out dissenting voices," Browning advised. A diverse team comprised of visionaries and task-oriented thinkers will be more cohesive and collaborative.

At Emergenetics, cognitive diversity is valued and employees are expected to contribute their unique perspectives. Browing wrote that it's the culture of not just valuing diversity, but expecting diversity, that's made the difference and led the company to greater success.

## Collaboration Mapping

Our workforce is still trying to shake the influences ingrained by the Industrial Era. For centuries, collaboration wasn't a common business practice. As a result, we still have much to learn about the practice of collaboration and how to use it as an effective business strategy.

One thing we know for sure, relationships aren't something that can be forced; rather, they tend to happen organically. It's possible for a leader to request collaboration or to think collaboration is happening in an area of the organization, when it's not. On the flipside, it's also possible for collaboration to be happening within the organization, yet no one knows it's happening.

Knowing where, when, and how collaboration happens in the organization is valuable information. For that reason, McKinsey & Company consulting firm recommends mapping the collaboration process in your organization by asking every employee questions about their interaction with other staff when making decisions, discussing new ideas, and working on projects.

With this information, your organization can begin to create a map illustrating the relationships and collaboration happening within the organization, start to measure how collaboration benefits the organization, and identify where the hurdles to collaboration exist.

Collaboration is an increasingly vital feature of business life. But when companies just promote collaboration, it doesn't always work. A collaborative map equips the organization with the information it needs to foster collaboration at the points where it delivers the best economic return. The following examples, each from different industries, illustrate the range of possibilities:

- In a nonprofit, collaboration mapping revealed the employees with the best track records for fundraising had strong relationships with donors and more connections within the nonprofit itself. It was determined tenure and experience both contributed to fundraising success. Meanwhile, new employees charged with fundraising quickly became frustrated and quit. By shifting strategies to help new employees replicate the networks of the most successful fundraisers, the nonprofit expected to increase its revenue by nearly 200 percent.

- For a construction company, collaboration mapping revealed the account managers in the highest-performing offices spent 68 percent more time with customers than account managers in other offices. The company replicated the process being used in its high-performing offices in its low-performing offices and observed revenue growth.

- An engineering company's collaboration map revealed a small number of employees single-handedly accounted for 35 percent of all the collaboration occurring within the company. By building connectivity throughout the entire organization, the firm raised its revenue to $275 million—up from $80 million—in a single year.

Often, organizations that operate without collaboration mapping allocate resources inefficiently, manage talent blindly, and experience large disparities in the effectiveness of collaboration within and across units. Studying the collaboration process and outcomes helps organizations make educated decisions about where to invest in additional connectivity and realize greater revenues as a result.

## Tribes

In the Industrial Era, work was a transaction, primarily revolving around a self-serving attitude. Workers would ask "What's In It For Me?," primarily concerned with the paycheck, title, job responsibilities, benefits, and bonus. Likewise, organizations would demand "What Will You Do For Us?," primarily concerned with how an employee's work would benefit the bottom line.

In the Talent Economy, there's ample research to support that a move to collaboration and a "What's In It For *We*" approach makes the most business sense. Some researchers believe the ultimate goal should be the development of a tribe; the stage when large groups of employees are so engaged and passionate about their workplace's environment and culture that they become protective of it. Dave Logan, Ph.D., John King, and Halee Fischer-Wright, M.D. studied 24,000 people in two dozen companies over the course of ten years, discovering extraordinary jumps in productivity and profitability occur when positive workplace tribes are formed.

However, tribes tend to form over a shared emotion—good or bad. Therefore, some tribes form over a shared resentment for their employer or a shared resistance to change. Needless to say, these tribes usually have the opposite effect on an organization's success, reducing morale and productivity, and fostering an organization-wide culture of apathy and negativity.

The researchers identified five types of tribes, from the most toxic to the most engaged. If you want to know what stage a tribe is in, simply walk around the workplace and listen to how employees talk about the company and interact with one another. Shared language is the primary indicator of a tribe's presence and status.

Where does your organization place in the tribe structure?

- **Stage One**
  These tribes are distinguished by hostility and despair. Their members say things like "This company is the worst."

- **Stage Two**
  These tribes are characterized by apathy. They don't try, they don't care, they don't innovate, they don't hold one another accountable for anything, and they revel in their disengagement. Their members say things like "My job is the worst" or "Management is a bunch of idiots," or "Nothing will ever change."

- **Stage Three**
  Tribal members are selfish and personally competitive at this stage, extremely averse to collaboration. The most common words they use are "I," "me," and "my." They say things like "I have an idea. I have a plan to turn this group around, and I hope you'll join me in leading this turnaround." Their attitude is "I'm great, and you're not."

- **Stage Four**
  Tribe members have a sense of shared values; they willingly

share knowledge and collaborate. These tribes are extremely competitive, and their competitive focus is on other companies. These tribes say, "We're great, and they're not."

- **Stage Five**

  Tribes that attain this level are characterized by a sense of happiness and amazement. They are highly innovative and collaborative, applying themselves to the creation of things no one has dreamed of—and are frequently incredibly successful in doing so. These tribes are mission-centric and inspired, often saying "Work is great. Life is great."

The next time you're around a group of coworkers, listen closely to the language they use. If you hear things like "This is awful," or "I have more experience," or "This will change the world" over and over, you'll have a pretty good idea of the state of that tribe.

The researchers discovered the commonality of language distinguished the groups that were successful from the ones that weren't. Stage Five teams outperform Stage Four teams, which outperform Stage Three, and so on. In fact, Stage Four tribes reported a 3,000 percent increase in profitability over groups at Stage Three. (Yes, you read that right: 3,000 percent.) Good news! The researchers found that it is possible to change the tribe's stage.

For example, if you're working with a Stage Two tribe, find the people who want things to be different; the ones who are tired of the griping. Then talk Stage Three language to them individually. Saying things like, "I think you have real potential to lead. I think that you could go a long way toward improving things here." If you've chosen the right person, then eventually she'll look at her colleagues and say, "You're right! I'm great, and this situation is awful." Moving just one person to Stage Three makes a difference, because that person will begin to use Stage Three language with others.

Initially, researchers found that Stage Five was difficult to maintain and very few organizations could reach it. This was largely because Stage Five tribes tend to produce things that disrupt their industry. These tribes change the world and can achieve things that are inconceivable for groups simply aiming to outperform the competition. They can move into a realm of pure creativity, leadership, and innovation. They say, "Let's do it because it's possible and we think it will change the world."

However, as their decade of research progressed, the researchers became convinced that society was moving into an era when Stage Five companies would become the norm, because disruption, entrepreneurism, and innovation were the norm. In fact, when their research concluded, the researchers predicted Stage Five companies would become so common, they would represent the future of business—further proof that the Industrial Era has come to an end.

MemberClicks is an example of a successful tribe. For the membership software company comprised of 52 employees serving 1,600 organizations, collaboration is one of the pillars of the organization's culture, and has been since the company was founded in 1998. "The main values that we live and die by is autonomy and collaboration. The moment you realize as a leader you can't solve all the problems, especially as you grow and the world around you gets more disruptive, that's when you realize it requires a village," explained Mark Sedgeley, CEO.

Collaboration is so important to MemberClicks, the company doesn't allow staff to work remotely. Yet, about 75 percent of the MemberClicks team are Millennials.

In a previous chapter, I mentioned how Best Buy and Yahoo! fell under scrutiny for eliminating the option for employees to work remotely. Part of this scrutiny stemmed from the fact that both organizations changed their minds, offering remote workplaces then reversing their decisions a few years later. The commitment to collaboration works at MemberClicks, which wants staff to come into the office and, well, collaborate.

"We have a lot of perks here, but they align directly with our values. I'm not offering a remote workforce. I'm not offering 30 day sabbaticals. I don't do any of that stuff. That's not in alignment with our values. Does that rule some people out to come work for me? Absolutely," Sedgley said, adding that staying true to the company's values ensures that the employees who do engage, do so because they engage in what MemberClicks stands for and they see value in it.

Collaboration is core to the MemberClicks employee experience, and the team engages in considerable team-building and dialogue about why their work is important and how to better serve their clients. "I feel I am contributing to something. I know why I'm doing what I'm doing so it just makes me feel connected to the rest of the company," said Kallie Walker, inbound marketing specialist, and a Millennial employee.

"In some other companies if you're younger, you're viewed as incapable. But here everyone is given a lot of responsibility and you're expected to perform at a really high level regardless of what your age is or what your role is. It's really refreshing, honestly, to be given that responsibility because that's not just handed to you anywhere else."

Kenzie Mayham, head of upgrade teams and another Millennial employee, said she feels like she's part of a family and part of a cause at MemberClicks. "That really motivates me to keep pushing myself forward and in turn, that pushes the organization forward," she said.

Focusing on why the company exists, conveying the importance of each employee's contribution to the company's mission, as well as placing a high value on teamwork and collaboration have all contributed to the company's success and given it a competitive advantage. "We see the trends. We hear the feedback and we adapt," Sedgley explained, noting that the team benefits from the collaboration that takes place between experienced employees and new employees.

Turnover remains low, even among their Millennial team. "Because we all know what we're doing and why we're doing it, it makes us more involved, a little bit more passionate about it and more tied to the company. You don't really want to leave because you're so involved in that project," explained Walker.

In keeping true to its collaborative culture, MemberClicks hires for culture and for mission, not for skills. Sedgley said the only way to manage through change and keep pace is to build a team composed of people who are centered on the company's mission, values, and willing to keep it alive. Other entities will struggle to adapt, roll with the tide, and eventually fall behind, he said.

Shawn Riegsecker is another Talent Economy pioneer. I met him back in 2009 and his pure dedication and drive to build an amazing company left a lasting impression on me. For starters, Riegsecker built Centro, a Chicago-based media management software company comprised of 700 employees, entirely on the importance of collaboration and teamwork.

Since the company's founding in 2001, Riegsecker, CEO, has put people first to create more fun, innovation, connection and transparency, which has allowed Centro to "create a level of human connection that I don't think exists in many companies," he said.

At Centro, each employee is responsible for their own improvement, the improvement of those around them, and the improvement of the company. They are also expected to live by 11 principles including courage, humility, honesty, and accountability.

Riegsecker explained that each employee understands and feels a connection to the Centro mission and knows how they personally fit into the big picture. "People want to know that the work they are doing is meaningful and are much more likely to be engaged if they believe that the work they do matters," he said.

## Wheel of Effectiveness

This exercise was adapted from one I co-developed with change management author Laura Goodrich. It's featured in our online course "Millennials to Members" but certainly applies here.

Complete the wheel based on your current level of effectiveness in each of the following categories. The small circles represent a scale of 1 to 8 (1 being very adept, 8 being very challenging), starting at the edge of the wheel. If you are highly adept in a particular category, color in the circle closest to the word bubble, and if you struggle in the category, color in a circle closer to the center of the wheel. Then connect all your points to see how bumpy your wheel might be.

It's best if you color in a wheel for yourself, then do it again based on your organization's effectiveness in each category. This will clearly demonstrate where more collaboration is needed.

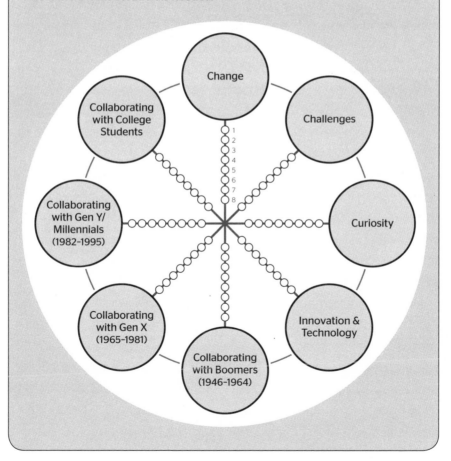

"Finally, and possibly most importantly, is that you have to make it fun. We simply spend too many hours of our life at the office for it not to be a fun place full of friends." By creating opportunities for employees to develop personal relationships with one another, Riegsecker said Centro has not only enriched their personal lives, but made them more invested in the company, as well.

## A Greater Mission

Collaboration has been proven to help recruit, retain, and motivate employees; increase productivity; bring new products and services to the market faster; increase customer satisfaction and loyalty; and improve an organization's bottom line. And because it lowers stress, it makes for a better work environment overall. Collaboration is not the same as teamwork or cooperation, but an organization-wide cultural value that should be embedded in the company's fabric.

In the Industrial Era, collaboration was considered extra work. In the Talent Economy, collaboration is what work is all about. In the Talent Economy, new perspectives and varied skillsets can make almost any idea happen.

Perhaps one of the most inspirational stories of collaboration comes from Amanda Haddock. In 2015, Haddock was honored as a White House Champion of Change for Precision Medicine. When her son was diagnosed with an aggressive brain cancer in 2010, there were few effective treatments, and after only 20 months, at 18 years old, he passed away.

Haddock and her husband started volunteering with brain cancer groups almost as soon as their son was diagnosed, and in his honor, continued volunteering after his death. At one of those events, a cancer researcher said in her speech that she thought a cure for cancer could be found if they could compare 50,000 genomes.

That sentence stuck with Haddock and her husband. "We couldn't figure out why someone wasn't comparing those genomes. As soon as she finished speaking, we asked to talk with her. She explained to us that although there are many genome databases, none of them had reached a scale large enough to do the types of comparisons she thought was necessary," Haddock wrote in an article following her White House Champion designation.

Haddock started researching, searching for the biggest genomic databases she could find, and talking to as many researchers as she could. "The recurring theme always seemed to be that none of the databases included everything that the researchers wanted. There were major technological hurdles of sharing and collaborating on large scale amounts of genomic data. Nothing we could find was built to scale to the vision of collaborative research that we had formed," she wrote.

Haddock and her husband envisioned a new kind of real-time, open-access infrastructure incorporating genomic and clinical data, which would be accessible to anyone working on cancer research— but they couldn't find anyone who believed that a collaborative database was possible.

So they took matters into their own hands. In 2013, they launched a nonprofit focused on giving cancer researchers the tools and technology they need to find better treatments and cures. Initially partnering with a group of pediatric cancer researchers and a consortium of research hospitals, Haddock started creating an open access data repository, allowing for new types of collaborative analyses to be performed on the internet. She continues to work to create a database where hospitals, medical schools, and nonprofit organizations can add and share molecular, genetic, clinical and environmental data related to brain cancer. Via collaboration, Haddock and her husband's efforts have the capacity to transform not only cancer research, but also any number of other biomedical research fields.

President Obama's idea was to bring in top talent from Silicon Valley, creating a way for government and technology to collaborate and solve some of the nation's problems. The United States Digital Service (USDS) became the federal government's go-to group for modernizing outdated procedures and systems.

In a report to Congress, the USDS claimed numerous wins, such as speeding up veterans' disability claims, streamlining immigrants' green cards, securing citizen's tax information, and running a bug bounty program—a competition to find and fix software glitches—for the Pentagon.

Of course, USDS' biggest win was likely the open-enrollment season for Healthcare.gov, which went smoothly in the years following the 2013 debacle. That was a big accomplishment, but USDS didn't receive any coverage of it because there was nothing to say. The site worked. Mission accomplished.

As the Healthcare.gov rescue effort demonstrated—or, indeed, any successful collaboration can prove—people working together towards a common goal with a common mission can have a profound and lasting effect.

**CHAPTER SUMMARY**

Collaboration is often seen as an activity that involves team members working on a project together. True collaboration isn't limited to doing one project or something that's done every once in a while; it is a strategy which maximizes individual contribution while leveraging the collective intelligence of everyone involved.

In a truly collaborative environment, everyone has a voice (always) and contributes (continually). When people understand how their contributions fit into the organization's strategy, it gives them purpose. With that purpose comes belief and trust in the organization, its leaders, and co-workers. Purpose and belief translate into higher levels of employee engagement.

At the most basic level, people want to feel a sense of belonging. For this reason, collaboration should take center stage in every organization because, more than anything else, it creates an environment in which employees feel like they belong.

**QUESTIONS TO CONSIDER**

1. In which areas of your organization would more collaboration prove beneficial?

2. How could collaboration benefit you personally?

3. How could collaboration benefit your organization?

4. What steps can you take in the next 30 days towards increased collaboration?

5. If your organization is a membership association, what collaborative tools and resources could you provide to benefit member companies or advance an entire industry?

*Organizations in the final phase of Talent Generation will seek ways to resolve what caused our talent crisis in the first place, aligning business with education, focusing on workforce and leadership development, and seeking to create a better future for all.*

*"The most valuable asset this country has is not gold or oil, but the minds of young people."*

DR. IRVING FRADKIN

CHAPTER 7

# Build a Better Future

Accounting graduates are in high demand. The U.S. Bureau of Labor Statistics predicts the profession will grow 11 percent during the next few years. *U.S. News & World Report* ranks accounting among the best jobs based on hiring demand, salary, and work-life balance. In Ohio, starting salaries in accounting are on the rise.

These stats should put the Ohio Society of CPAs at ease, but this is an organization that thinks a generation ahead. Through on-going dialogue with young professionals and accounting firm owners, their team kept hearing about skills gaps and the projected impact of retirements. Then research indicated Ohio's workforce was shrinking, with a projected 11 percent drop in high school graduates by 2031.

All these trends influenced the association's decision to pivot. "We have a significant workforce development issue and time is not on our side," explained Scott Wiley, President & CEO. "Boomers are retiring and fewer Millennials are joining the accounting workforce. In member surveys, talent management is the top business challenge."

In 2016—three years after taking the helm—Wiley switched the entire association's focus. Resources, products, services, mission, vision, and brand were revamped to focus on advancing and diversifying the profession, a switch-up with a strong emphasis on workforce development.

Wiley said he realized the association had a vital role to play in bridging demand and supply. There's not enough talent to keep the industry afloat, and there was no other organization equipped to collaborate, innovate, and ultimately solve Ohio's accounting talent generation problem. So, Wiley repurposed Ohio Society of CPAs to take the challenge on.

## Workforce Development

As I'm writing this book, the nation is recovering from the Clinton-Trump presidential campaign, one of the most rigorous battles for president in history between the first female presidential candidate and the first presidential candidate with no prior political or military experience. (Yet another indicator we are witnessing a world of change.)

I will leave it up to the pundits to dissect the political ramifications coming out of this election, but at the end of the day our political leaders have a job to do, especially when it comes to establishing important public policy to solve the skills gap and craft a workforce development strategy. Actually, we all have a job to do. We can't just sit back wait on our government to fix this problem. It's too far-reaching, too urgent, and too significant. Workforce development is not a new issue. Workforce development started to become an issue in the late 1960s, when demographers realized that the generation of children being born—Generation X—was a much smaller population by comparison to the Baby Boomer generation. There were concerns then about talent development, mostly due to the differences in population sizes.

Today, we're not only concerned about population, we're also concerned about skills gaps, the diversification of jobs, the evolution of technology, the urbanization of America—all factors that come into question when we think about talent generation.

If we want to build a growing economy for generations to come, every organization has a role to play—be it a business, nonprofit, school, membership association, or government entity. We all must work to solve the skills gap and develop a strong foundation for today's workforce and generations to come.

## A City View

In the early 2000s I worked as the director of communications and media relations for the Minneapolis Regional Chamber of Commerce. At the time, there were concerns about attracting businesses to the city and Minneapolis engaged in a branding campaign to promote its quality of life (and downplay the region's winter weather).

Fast forward 17 years, cities aren't just trying to attract businesses, they're trying to attract talent. This is how we know the war for talent has intensified, because cities and states are advertising for talent, encouraging individuals to relocate and work there. Open any business or in-flight magazine, and you see ads promoting Louisiana, Florida, and Kansas to prospective workers and employers alike.

In 2007, urban dwellers surpassed 50 percent of the total global population, and that proportion is expected to grow to more than 70 percent by 2050. As urban economic growth expands, tier-two cities will begin to stagnate and shrink. As a result, cities now play an important role in workforce development. The cities that avoid a disappearing act will be those that invest in marketing and inspire pride in their citizens.

## Marketing

Naveen Rajdev is the chief marketing officer of Wipro, a global digital marketing company. In an article in *Forbes*, Rajdev said it's time for cities to think of their citizens as customers. Customers have choices.

If they don't like a product, then they won't buy it. The same is true of residents. Plenty of cities exist in the world, so if people don't like living in one, or don't have access to the careers they desire, then they will happily move to another.

This means cities need to think of themselves as businesses and market their cities to companies, residents, and prospects alike. After all, the most popular cities have a global recognition of their cultures in the same way that businesses create their own company cultures. Does "What Happens in Vegas Stays in Vegas" ring a bell?

ChooseATL was a marketing campaign that evolved from a taskforce of Atlanta's biggest brands, startup leaders, government representatives, and nonprofit partners. Concerned about the wave of Boomer retirements and pending shortage of skilled labor and desiring to compete for talent with regions like Silicon Valley, the grassroots movement was designed to position the city as a digital hub ideal for high-tech minded newcomers, prospective entrepreneurs, and residents of the creative class.

The campaign features a video series and website showcasing Atlanta's culture and business climate, entrepreneurs and other local talent, highlighting what makes its citizens so proud, and identifying what volunteer efforts can do for the city.

### Technology

In addition to marketing, cities should embrace technology and digitize public processes and interfaces to simplify residents' lives. For example, Atlanta hosts an annual Govathon, a citywide hackathon which focuses on resolving problems that affect the local government and the community.

Consider the example of Barcelona, Spain. A few years ago Barcelona's mayor formed a team tasked with identifying new opportunities to enhance services for the city's people and businesses. Smart City Barcelona identified 12 areas for intervention and initiated

22 programs. These innovations yielded significant cost savings, improved the quality of life for residents, and made the city a center for the young tech industry. Plus, Barcelona's fiber network now provides 90 percent fiber-to-the-home coverage, serves as a backbone for integrated city systems, and provides citywide Wi-Fi. Today, Barcelona is considered the world's most wired city.

Cities can aid in workforce development, but that will require a change-up in their own Industrial Era processes. Presently, most cities use marketing or economic development agencies to create packages and encourage investment, or they leave messaging to business consortiums and communications officers. Others rely on public relations efforts. But PR plans don't usually take into consideration the consumer experience, such as what residents think of the city, how that city should be placed in comparison with others like it, or whether businesses and talent will stick around.

To positively influence workforce development, cities must establish a desired experience for potential talent. As Rajdev put it: "A city's name shouldn't be a noun; it should be an adjective that encompasses a culture."

The *Sacramento Business Journal* posted news videos addressing the city's workforce development challenges. The Greater Rochester Chamber of Commerce created an Office of Future Leadership to focus on workforce development among young professionals.

From coast to coast and beyond, workforce development has emerged as every city's challenge and opportunity. Here are some other examples of how cities are approaching workforce development:

### Nashville: Groom Young Talent

Also known as Music City, Nashville has a continual influx of musical, creative, and entrepreneurial talent largely driven by the Millennial generation. The city boasts 60 percent retention of college graduates from the area's 20+ colleges and universities. This graduate retention exceeds peer cities, noted Alex Hughes, Vice President of Talent Attraction & Retention at Nashville Area Chamber of Commerce.

However, an estimated 120,000–140,000 individuals will be retiring from the Nashville region's workforce in the next five years, and only 90,000–110,000 high school and college students will be entering the workforce during that same timeframe. The region is also anticipating an additional 40,000–50,000 migrant workers to enter the labor market, with the majority having prior experience.

"Our focus will be on attracting and growing the middle-skill talent pool, which is where we will see the biggest pinch, particularly in advanced manufacturing and trade-related occupations," Hughes said.

YP Nashville is trying to tackle the workforce challenge. The partnership between the Nashville Area Chamber of Commerce and 50 young professional organizations works to engage, connect, and empower young professionals to actively shape the future of the Nashville region.

"This initiative is solely focused on building the next generation of leaders," Hughes explained. The initiative includes the Nashville Emerging Leader Awards program and provides young professionals with opportunities to collaborate, share ideas, gain support, and influence community leadership on a broader scale.

### Austin: Youth Workforce Programs

It's not common for a city to be listed among great places to work, but in 2016 the city ranked 22 on *Forbes'* list of America's Best Employers, making it the top-rated public service entity on the list. Austin, the capital of Texas, is the eleventh largest city in the nation. It has more than 12,000 municipal employees working in more than 20 departments.

In the 1970s, IBM built a facility in Austin. Since then, several technology companies have established roots in Austin and the city of Austin has found itself competing for talent with Facebook, Dell, Google, and Apple.

The City of Austin realized it had to stay on top of its game to compete against other companies in the region. The City also realized that if it wanted to effectively serve the citizens and businesses of Austin, it needed to build a great workplace for itself.

Sonja Alexander-Harry, Senior Business Process Consultant for the City of Austin, said the City takes into consideration how it builds its own talent and how it helps the City's companies engage talent, as well.

In the 1980s, Alexander-Harry's first job as a teenager was working for the City of Austin. She's held roles in other government entities, but noted these other entities were neither collaborative nor inclusive. She eventually returned to work for the City in 2004. What's unique about working for the City of Austin, she explained, is the clarity of mission and each employee's role in supporting that mission.

"Since the beginning, even when I worked for the City as a teenager, I knew my role and the operation of the department. Alignment is clear and so is the goal of what we're trying to accomplish. Every project at the City starts with, "You're needed to complete the project and here's why," and the project's goals are outlined. The expected deliverable is clear," Alexander-Harry said.

"The work of the city is meaningful work. There's a sense of accomplishment and understanding how we each affect the bottom line. The management structure is very collab-orative to address the issues the city faces."

The City of Austin is committed to being the most family friendly city in the country, and this commitment is realized through structures and policies that engage the participation of young people, which is another way the City is helping to solve the workforce development issue. Alexander-Harry noted this exceptional commitment to developing future talent differentiates the City from other public service entities in the United States.

Here are just a few of the youth workforce initiatives the City offers:

- Composed of 85 high school students, the Austin Youth Council meets once a month to discuss issues concerning youth and listen to presentations from City staff and other organizations in the city.

- AustinCorps is a civic education and leadership development program for high school students. Combining classroom curriculum on local government with a hands-on experience at City Hall, students meet with city policy-makers and administrators, complete a mentored internship with the city, and work in small groups to plan and execute a community project.

In addition, there are STEM occupation, aviation department, and Austin Convention Center summer internship programs, plus youth employment opportunities in 12 departments including animal services, police, water, and energy departments.

Despite the city's achievements, Alexander-Harry said the City never stops innovating. "If you're stagnant, your organi-zation will eventually die out or become inefficient. You must be open to change. The demand for change will only increase. At the City of Austin, we realize we will continually have to work smarter, work faster, manage our priorities, and be open to change."

### Hickory: Community Collaboration

Once known as the furniture capital of the world, Hickory, North Carolina emerged from the 2009 recession in rough shape. "Our number one business issue is attracting young people to manufacturing jobs. It's at a crisis stage. We have 3,000 jobs that go unfilled every day," explained Danny Hearn, former president and CEO of the Catawba County Chamber of Commerce in Hickory.

A couple years ago, the chamber literally brought young professionals to the decision-making table. The chamber's board, previously composed almost entirely of seasoned executives, was revamped so at least half were professionals under the age of 40.

In addition, the chamber started engaging young professionals in the creation of videos about employment opportunities to creatively promote job openings at local employers to their peers.

The chamber also launched *Made Magazine,* an online and print publication, featuring information about advanced manufacturing and other jobs in the Catawba region. Community leaders wanted to showcase the community and career opportunities to prospective young employees. For its inaugural issue, advertising oversold by 33 percent and 25,000 copies were distributed to schools, community organizations, and parents.

Recognizing that engaging young professionals was an urgent need for many local organizations, the chamber also reached out to area YMCAs, Rotary Clubs, and faith groups to share information, ideas, and collaboratively create strategies focused on retaining young talent in the region.

Seen as a visionary leader in the community, closely aligned with young professionals and community leaders, the Chamber improved member retention, growing from 83 percent in 2011 to 92 percent in 2015. Hearn feels pride in what has been accomplished, and is enthusiastic about the future of Catawba County Chamber and the Hickory region. "I know our organization and the community will be in good hands for generations to come," he said.

### London: Invest in the Tech Sector

An estimated 40,000 tech businesses are in London, employing almost 200,000 people, or 3.5 percent of the capital's total workforce. Despite this success, there is a growing gap between the skills young Londoners have and those that digital and technology businesses in the capital need if they are to continue to thrive.

London's mayor wants to bridge this gap to ensure young Londoners are taught the digital skills they need to access well-paid jobs, while companies recruit local talent. In 2016, Mayor Sadiq Khan pledged £7m to support the city's technology and digital industries with talent.

The Digital Talent Program was created to provide 1,500 young Londoners with access to industry-backed training, internships, and jobs. A portion of the funding will be directed toward the development of new programs at schools, which will be designed in collaboration with London's high-tech employers.

"It is vital that we nurture the next generation of digital enthusiasts so we can continue to provide our tech firms with home-grown talent," stated Khan in an interview. "Our vibrant tech sector is globally renowned and the city is awash with thousands of tech innovators and entrepreneurs who are developing the latest apps and software and delivering economic prosperity for the city. It is vital that we nurture the next generation of digital enthusiasts so we can continue to provide our tech firms with home-grown talent."

## An Industry's Responsibility

Cities are tackling the workforce development challenge, and so are industries. Here are perspectives from leaders in two very different industries—osteopathic medicine and energy—who are observing workforce development from very different approaches.

### Growing Younger

"Osteopathic medicine has taken an interesting turn. There was a huge increase in the number of osteopathic medical schools about 25 years ago and the actual population of osteopathic physicians has grown by 300 percent in 20 years," explained Adrienne White-Faines, CEO of the American Osteopathic Association (AOA). As a result, 65 percent of the osteopathic physicians are under the age of 45.

"AOA was originally designed for a small, older generation of osteopathic physicians who came up in a very different healthcare environment," she said. "Now, the vast majority of the physicians in osteopathic medicine are Gen X and Millennials."

White-Faines was appointed CEO in 2013, after AOA realized it needed to "redesign and realign," she said. While AOA doesn't have a workforce development problem, per se, it's still a challenge to create an organization that keeps pace with the Talent Economy and meets the needs of a rapidly changing workforce. It's workforce development concerns are not focused on recruiting individuals, but on retaining and serving the talent that's already there.

White-Faines said the first step she took towards rebuilding AOA as an industry resource was to spend time envisioning the future; not just a few years out, but at least a decade. This practice helped the organization's leaders see the need for and warm up to the idea of change. "If you're feeling anxious about change, start by envisioning the organization 10 to 15 years from now. It helps you to see the future and understand where change needs to happen now."

After visioning, AOA's leaders realized the path they were on now wouldn't get them to where they needed to be. "It was very, very clear that our present and future were misaligned," White-Faines said.

From there, AOA created a strategy to "get us from where we are to where we need to be." The strategy is broken into phases, some of which take three to five years to implement. "For me, the first two years after I was named CEO were really building the story, building the culture, building the argument, building the paradigm, articulating the need for change and helping people to visualize what the change should be," White-Faines said.

AOA spent three years on achieving the first phase, making what White-Faines refers to as "significant and monumental changes" specific to positioning. AOA is now in its second phase of reaching its vision, which is dedicated toward redesigning member services.

"We recognized that we were not relevant to our members—this younger generation—and that we were losing membership. But redesigning member services and member relevance needed to come in phase two, because you can't move people or argue or build toward member relevance if you don't have the services in place first," White-Faines explained.

So far, AOA has focused on building up the areas that interest younger generations, modernizing many areas of the association and positioning it in "more modern markets and in stronger social media platforms."

Presently, AOA is reviewing its governance to eliminate a process based on longevity and hierarchy and appointment. AOA was previously home to "bureaus" of student leaders, resident leaders, and young physicians. Each of these groups met separately but were not part of any other area in the association.

"If you were interested in research or if you were interested in public health, you didn't sit on the Bureau of Public Health, you were designated as a student, you sat on the Bureau of Student Affairs," White-Faines explained. AOA realized this was creating more silos and not engaging young people at a time when collaboration, community-building, and workforce development were critical.

Being a part of AOA means knowing what's going on in healthcare and understanding how to shape it, she said. With 65 percent of AOA's population falling into the young physician category, AOA needed the voice and perspective of the younger physicians represented within every area of the organization.

"It's a very similar problem that organizations have had historically with diversity. The typical response is, 'Oh, yes. We need diversity. Let's have a council of minority affairs, or let's have a council of women.'" White-Faines said the era of "putting people in a corner to sit and look at themselves and have no influence" must come to an end. AOA eliminated its Council of Minority Affairs, Council of Student Affairs, and Council of Residents. "We said, 'In every area, make sure there are women, make sure there's racial diversity, make sure there are students and age diversity, and make sure there's geographic diversity. That's the way that you service a nationwide organization.'"

With at least 30 percent of the voices in the room being from individuals who have been in practice less than five years, it "totally changes the dialogue" and is effective at engaging young people, White-Faines said. She also recommends hiring interns. "I highly, highly advocate that hiring interns is one of the best ways to bring in fresh innovative ideas. You will learn from them and the interns will learn from you."

Although AOA is representing an industry that's actually growing younger rather than older, White-Faines said the need for change and the demand for excellence is always there. "There's not a tolerance anymore for organizations that don't consistently exude excellence. ... It's now about, can you consistently deliver on excellence, constantly innovate, constantly commit to be better? The organizations that do that are going to survive."

## Growing Older

In stark contrast to osteopathic medicine, the energy industry isn't getting younger—it's getting older. Katie Mehnert, CEO of Pink Petro, a career platform for women in the energy industry, wants to change that reality and attract the next generation into the industry. In fact, Pink Petro just formed a collaboration with the World Economic Forum.

As a second-generation industry professional, Mehnert sees the industry struggling to survive and has made it her mission to be a vehicle of workforce development for the industry.

In 2016, Pink Petro, in collaboration with KCA and gleXnet, conducted an industry research project titled Energy 2021. The study proved that the oil and gas industry is facing a crisis on multiple fronts: Regulation, market volatility, OPEC policies, external perception, and an aging workforce have created a perfect storm.

"The crew change is on. We've been talking about it. Twenty years ago when I entered the workforce we were talking about it. We knew we'd have this massive amount of people retire at some point," Mehnert said. Retirements had been delayed until "a market event hit a couple of years ago and oil started crashing" and companies accelerated their plans to move people into new roles.

Mehnert said the energy industry's workforce woes have been in the making for decades. In the 1980s, students were discouraged from pursuing careers in energy because hiring slowed significantly. "We stopped hiring engineers. We stopped pipelining talent. And it's one thing to get a computer programmer and it's another thing to get somebody who can touch and deal with hydrocarbons all day long," she said. "We didn't hire people and we're paying for that now."

As a result, the industry is staring down a significant shortage of talent, plus a competency gap. Mehnert said the industry has no choice but to focus on training, industry coaching, and recruiting people from outside the industry.

When asked about how to resolve the workforce development crisis, Mehnert said the first step is to change the conversation. Literally. "Oil and gas, utilities—the energy industry powers everything we do. But we don't talk about that. The only stories Millennials and others hear about are when we blow things up, or when we screw up, or when we harm the environment," she explained. In the past, education and communication were usually reactive, at least in the energy industry, and Mehnert wants it to shift to being proactive.

"The energy industry has a hard time attracting new talent, because no one really understands what we do," she said, adding that it's imperative for industry leaders to educate outsiders about the jobs, but also how good it feels to power the world. "My hope is that I can take industry and the mainstream, and bring them a little closer together. That's the first thing we do, is to help tell the stories."

Mehnert noted the energy industry "is about 30 years behind." She believes this delay has directly contributed to the industry's workforce challenge, as many energy companies are just beginning to think about having conversations with the next generation.

The next step, according to Mehnert, is to conduct outreach to those previously affected by down cycles or absent from the industry altogether—women and minorities in particular. "We need to attract new people to the industry and we need to help them find jobs," she said. "We've got to find new feeder pools for talent, and we've got to go after those aggressively." To that point, in 2017 Pink Petro is launching the Experience Energy talent platform to help companies find talent for contract, full time, and executive opportunities in the energy sector.

The third step is to create widespread awareness and engage others in helping to solve the workforce crisis. In 2016, Pink Petro hosted the HERWorld Energy Forum, which drew in 5,000 attendees and was broadcast in 40 countries. The forum bills itself as an innovative and inclusive learning event that addresses new frontiers in the energy industry.

Slowly but surely, Mehnert is gaining traction and changing the fate of the energy industry. Her partnership with the World Economic Forum is focused on ending the gender gap in the industry. But there's still work to do. Presently, Mehnert has been focused on recruiting talent. The next hurdle will be talent retention.

"Honestly, what keeps me up at night is wondering: how are we going to engage the Millennial generation? This work is not something you learn in six weeks' time and we have to get people to be proficient and competent very quickly," she explained. Unlike most professions, this industry's work can be complicated, challenging, and even life-threatening. Considerable change looms on the horizon, with artificial intelligence, robots, and more digital influences, as well.

Mehnert has learned, especially from her experience working in the energy industry, that change is the new norm and ignoring it will be hugely detrimental—potentially for decades. She said she will continue to call upon the industry to learn, collaborate, and prioritize workforce development.

"Learning is what accelerates change. If the industry is going to stay relevant, and if companies are going to stay relevant, they need to learn from their customers and their competitors and find ways to collaborate," she said. "And leaders need to be prepared to prepare not just themselves, their peers, and the company—but the workforce as well."

As you will notice from these city and industry examples, the perfect recipe for workforce development doesn't exist. That's because workforce development has never been a problem of this magnitude, breadth, or severity. The switch over to the Talent Economy, mixed with the largest shift in human capital in history, has formed a perfect storm. Our workforce needs have forever shifted, and every entity everywhere is struggling to adapt, engage, and grow talent. Those entities that step up to solve the problem will be the ones that survive.

## Leadership Development

Workforce development is a pressing issue, and sliding in at a close second is leadership development. With each passing day, Millennial leaders assume an increasing role in steering both the nation's economy and the organizations that comprise it. The number of them moving into the C-suite is only going to increase over this next decade—making it even more important to understand how their leadership perspectives differ, as well as best practices for teaching them leadership skills.

The Conference Board, Development Dimensions International, and RW2 Enterprises interviewed and surveyed employees in various leadership roles and age ranges at 14 organizations. The research brought to light a key generational difference: Millennials think leaders should be nimble, relational and collaborative, while older generations think leaders should have efficient decision-making skills and business acumen. In addition, the Millennial-aged leaders favored informal employer-employee relationships more than their older counterparts, as well as being given outcomes for measuring goals.

This isn't surprising, considering Millennials represent the Talent Economy, and other generations represent the Industrial Era. The fact is, the leadership style of Millennial leaders contrasts sharply with the style of Xers and Boomers. It's not about right or wrong—it's simply different. But when differences are ignored, this can create ever-widening gaps in the organization, prohibiting teamwork and collaboration.

There's nothing wrong with having a team dialogue about how different generations have different definitions of what makes a good leader. If organizations turn a blind eye to these differences, both the new, young leaders and the seasoned CEOs will become frustrated. This internal struggle is likely to wreak havoc on employee retention, morale, and productivity.

Differences aside, teaching leadership skills is often an overlooked or neglected necessity. "We must prepare young people to lead," stated John Baldoni. "Leadership development is not a program. It's a priority, and it needs to be part of every organization's DNA." Baldoni has consistently been listed among the top 30 leadership experts in the world and he's the author of thirteen books on the leadership topic. He elaborated on the urgency of leadership development.

"Today's leaders value experience in a safe environment because they haven't been trained to deal with disruption or being displaced. As a result, we see leaders coasting; just doing the minimum to get by. Plus, we live in a culture of success. This encourages leadership aspiration, but we don't study or explore how leaders got into leadership in the first place or how to develop other leaders," he explained.

This heralds back to some of the leadership challenges outlined in Chapter 2. The vast majority of today's leaders learned how to manage, but not how to lead, and there's a clear difference between the two. It's understanding that the leadership skills required in the Talent Economy differ from those in the Industrial Era. Moreover, it's realizing that young people have valuable skills to offer and leadership is starting younger than ever before, and we must adapt to these changes and prepare the next generation to lead.

As Baldoni points out, thinking about, planning for, and equipping future leaders is now an imperative and requires consistency to be successful. "Leadership is not just a title anymore, and it's not limited to just the oldest generation. Leadership is now a responsibility for everyone in the organization."

A challenge arises when Boomers retire, there's no pipeline or leadership strategy in place, and ambitious but inexperienced employees are tossed into leadership roles. This is especially challenging considering many organizations are still rooted in Industrial Era methodologies, which naturally creates gaps when you bring Talent Economy workers into the mix. However, as Boomers retire at an ever-increasing speed, organizations will need to prepare their Millennial employees to catch the ball and run.

Following are some tips for how to bridge the gap between two totally different economies and their corresponding generations.

| Xers and Boomers (Industrial Era) | Millennials (Talent Economy) |
| --- | --- |
| *Prefer managers who are well-educated, demonstrate good judgment, and have considerable on-the-job experience* | *Prefer to learn management by trial and error* |

**The Compromise:**
Identify company needs, match those needs to the person's interests, and make a plan.

An employee development plan, also known as career path, identifies the step-by-step process employees will take to acquire valuable skills. Career paths tend to fast-track the learning process. For example, an aspiring leader may first be asked to manage outside vendors and a budget associated with those vendors. Additional responsibilities are added as each step on the career path is mastered.

| Xers and Boomers (Industrial Era) | Millennials (Talent Economy) |
|---|---|
| *Just do it.* | *Why do I need to do this?* |

**The Compromise:**
Communicate why stretch assignments are needed,
how new tasks address skill gaps.

Millennials want to see the big picture. They want to understand the rationale behind assignments that stretch them to learn something new, and how doing so can lead to more responsibilities. Older generations, on the other hand, assume a sense of completion or accomplishment is enough to inspire employees to get the job done. Resolve this by communicating the big picture, including the how and the why of the assignment. Also, ask aspiring leaders to take the lead on team-building activities, engage them in role-play, research, mentorship, and hands-on learning experiences. These experiences will prepare them for future leadership opportunities.

| Xers and Boomers (Industrial Era) | Millennials (Talent Economy) |
|---|---|
| *Once a year feedback* | *Frequent feedback* |

**The Compromise:**
Create a system for regular feedback.

Schedule time for dialogue. The goal is to help your employees identify roadblocks and paths to move forward, so that they build confidence and experience. This is an especially valuable practice for aspiring leaders. Coach them through tough decisions by asking open-ended questions such as: "What was your reasoning behind that decision? Do you think it worked? Why or why not?" Make sure aspiring leaders know that you will check-in regularly to help keep them on track, remove roadblocks, and offer a sounding board. Also make sure they know you're not there to do the work for them, which will aid in building their confidence and autonomy.

## Raising Talent

The need for workforce development and leadership development begs a bigger question: Should we be raising talent rather than training it? Are our workforce development woes the result of a much bigger problem?

Despite being an up-and-coming, in-demand generation, and one that's consistently shaping how we think about work, Millennials are still having a hard time finding reasonable jobs. At the time this book is being written, the Millennial unemployment rate stands at an unfortunate 12.8 percent compared to the national average of 4.9 percent.

The modern American workplace needs Millennials to gain experience and replace previous generations—but they seem to be facing a uniquely difficult challenge doing so compared to other generations. In a survey by the Association of American Colleges and Universities, many employers believe recent college graduates are underdeveloped in key workplace skills like interpersonal communication, critical thinking, and organization. These are skills that aren't taught in higher education—there's no "general workplace skills" class in most universities. Instead, college students focus on theoretical studies in their respective disciplines. This makes it harder for Millennials, who believe themselves to be highly qualified, to land even the most basic jobs.

Workforce change has spurred considerable debate and discussion in recent years. Consider these stats:

- 16 percent of Americans think a four-year degree prepares students for a high-paying job in the modern economy— *Pew Research*

- 47 percent of existing jobs in America are susceptible to automation—*Oxford University*

- 55 percent decline in job openings for unskilled work between 2007 and 2015—*Massachusetts Institute of Technology*

- 49 percent of the highest paid job postings are seeking coding skills—*Burning Glass Technologies*

- 2,574 percent growth in demand for data-visualization skills since 2012—*Burning Glass Technologies*

- Since 2001, wages earned by workers with a Bachelor's degree have fallen more than the wages of high-school graduates— *New York Federal Reserve*

All these stats prove the need for education to evolve, and further indicate the important role education plays in workforce development.

Kevin Kruse has built and sold several technology companies. He researches and frequently writes about the topic of employee engagement. He wrote an article, published by Forbes titled "My Kids Are Straight A Students and They Know Nothing," in early 2017, bringing to light the lack of workforce training among young people, despite the fact they are the best educated generation in history.

Kruse isn't alone. Michael Toth, CEO of Learning Sciences International, has also sounded the alarm on education's role, or lack thereof, in workforce development. He authored an article voicing his concerns about teachers relying on teacher-centered instruction and lecture-recitation.

> We have moved rapidly from a manufacturing-centric economy to a global, technologically advanced, knowledge-based economy. Twenty first century employers are searching for workers who can analyze, problem-solve, communicate effectively and work in autonomous teams. We are preparing students for a world we can't even imagine. Do today's classrooms develop the analytical

and collaborative skills students need to enter the future with confidence? Are our classrooms truly rigorous? Unfortunately, we would have to say no. The data collected at Learning Sciences International suggests the majority of U.S. classrooms from primary to high school, even in advanced AP classes, are not supporting the level of cognitive complexity and student autonomy necessary to prepare students for the new economy workforce.[1]

However, some schools, teachers, and students are making the leap into a very different kind of learning environment; like a Loxahatchee, Florida elementary school. In every grade, students are using peer coaching, challenging each other for evidence, working in autonomous and collaborative teams, and taking responsibility for meeting their learning targets and achieving competency. Students review the state standards and work backwards to understand the skills they will need to meet the standards. Students aren't told what to do, but determine for themselves what needs to be accomplished to meet the standards.

Talent Economy classrooms are student-centered. Learning in these classrooms is rigorous, meaning higher cognitive complexity and higher student autonomy are both present. It's not just the content that is complex, but rather the level of complexity in student thinking. Students are routinely engaged in analysis, applying their analyses to real-world scenarios and inquiry-based problems. They are making decisions, learning to work effectively with peers, and holding themselves and their teams accountable for meeting learning targets.

Toth writes about how Talent Economy classrooms differ from other classrooms:

---

1 Reprinted with permission. SEEN Magazine. October 21, 2016. http://www.seenmagazine.us/Articles/Article-Detail/ArticleId/5929/Rigorous-Student-Centered-Classrooms-for-the-New-Economy

You see a lot of difference in the way the students talk. Kids asking each other, "Well, why do you think this?" And then, "Do you want to revise your thinking?" You'll hear this in first grade. They are using their peers as resources. And you'll hardly ever see a textbook, unless they're doing a foundational lesson.[2]

According to Toth, schools using student-centered learning report higher student scores—as much as double-digit increases within two years—as well as increased student participation in the classroom. Indeed, some schools are evolving education even as early as preschool, which previously focused on the basics of counting, learning the alphabet, and grasping basic social skills. Here are some new trends in education:

- **Coding**

  Some preschools are introducing technology literacy programs to teach computer coding. Early coding programs use elementary tools such as blocks and drawing to teach coding. Instead of drawing with a crayon, students are drawing with code. Is coding at four years old too early? Some think these skills should be learned at an older age, but fans of the concept think teaching children to code early on lends them more time to build on that skillset, potentially creating a generation that contains more highly educated computer scientists than we have now.

- **Creativity and STEAM**

  Combining creativity with technical skill development is part of a new trend in early childhood education. STEAM builds upon STEM's science, technology, engineering, and math curriculum by adding art into the mix. STEAM incorporates creative arts

---

2 Reprinted with permission. SEEN Magazine. October 21, 2016. http://www. seenmagazine.us/Articles/Article-Detail/ArticleId/5929/Rigorous-Student-Centered-Classrooms-for-the-New-Economy

within the fields, leading to opportunities for students to apply their hard science lessons in creative ways. The goal is to equip students for the workforce. For example, successful engineers need to be creative problem solvers to apply their technical expertise in new ways.

- **Life Skills**
Another trend emerging in education is the move towards teaching preschool students life skills, such as how to cook and garden. Students learn about the food chain and environmental issues such as food and water shortages, as well as sustainability.

While looking to preschool education as a barometer of future workforce trends isn't likely to be entirely accurate, it is something leaders should look to as they observe how future generations learn and work together. If there is no communication between business leaders and education leaders, we risk failing to prepare today's students for the best careers available. And without embracing the newest generation of workers, companies lose out on the latest skills that can benefit their businesses.

Here again, there isn't a universal recipe outlining what a school should do to prepare the next-generation workforce. We're learning this as we go, trying out new methodologies and researching different models. The point is, as with everything else, that what worked in the past isn't working anymore.

For decades, it has been believed that workforce success requires a college degree, and college requires a measurable set of abilities in key subjects. Students lacking in said subjects must focus on those weaknesses or else they will not succeed (graduate). This has been referred to as deficit-based teaching—focusing on a student's challenge in order to turn it into a strength. Focusing on a deficit brings a student's skill level up to average in order to pass the class.

But deficit-based teaching doesn't inspire excellence, which is cultivated entirely from strengths.

Think about it. If you are forced to master something that's difficult for you, you're likely to approach it with negativity, procrastination, or resentment. For me, it was algebra. It wasn't my strength. It was my kryptonite. And I haven't ventured anywhere near the stuff ever since.

People are passionate about what they're naturally good at, and most people get better at what they're good at because they are drawn to learning more about it and doing more of it. Passion breeds excellence. I would argue this is what students really need to succeed in the Talent Economy.

The answer seems simple enough. Revamp all education to be student-centered and future-focused. Align businesses with education to forge collaboration, provide students with strengths-based education, and ensure students are receiving the training and skills they need. Imagine your education providing access to internships and job shadowing and field trips to learn about different jobs and industries!

And the learning wouldn't stop there. To remain competitive, organizations of all types and sizes would give workers alike access to ongoing training and career-focused education. It's not a matter of mastery and meditation, but interactive experiences that expose employees to the continual learning of new skills.

In the Talent Economy, learning is critical to employee engagement and retention. According to Pew Research Center, 61 percent of all working Americans under the age of 30 think it's essential to develop new skills throughout their working lives. In fact, Manpower found that 93 percent of Millennials were willing to spend their own money on further training.

Our workforce—government, business, membership associations, and education entities—should consider what other countries are doing in regard to talent generation:

### Singapore

Concerned about the nation's aging and retiring workforce, the country's government launched several programs to support the nation's small and medium enterprises and prepare Singaporeans for the future economy.

The Committee on the Future Economy (CFE) was established by Singapore's government, composed of 30 members representing both large and small enterprises from different industries. The CFE established subcommittees to review and make recommendations on the Five Futures: Future Corporate Capabilities and Innovation, Future Growth Industries and Markets, Future of Connectivity, Future City, and Future Jobs and Skills.

One of Singapore's initiatives under this umbrella is SkillsFuture, a national movement to create a culture of lifelong learning and to help drive Singapore's next phase of workforce and economic development. All citizens ages 25 and older receive an initial SkillsFuture Credit of $500 from the government to pay for skills-related courses.

In addition to skills-related courses, the government provides access to leadership development and mentoring programs, internships, a work study program, management training, and career readiness programs for students.

The entire country of Singapore is focused on talent generation; being intentional about learning, skill development, employee engagement, and preparing the entire workforce for whatever the future may bring. It's an enviable feat because we're struggling in the United States to gain momentum behind the issue. We see a school, a company, or a region invest in the future, but it's far from being a national campaign or initiative.

### United Kingdom

The United Kingdom is taking steps toward talent generation as well.

In 2015, British Chambers of Commerce (BCC) surveyed 3,500 business and education leaders. Widespread media coverage and dialogue among the country's leaders ensued, as everyone was shocked to learn that 69 percent of respondents thought secondary schools were ineffective at preparing young people for careers, and 41 percent thought universities weren't preparing young people for employment, either.

In response to the findings, the BCC called for immediate business-to-education collaboration and a year later hosted the Business and Education Summit, bringing together senior leaders from both the education and business sectors to discuss how to best support young people's transition from education into the workplace.

Regardless of where you live or what industry you work in, talent generation (or a lack thereof) is influencing your life. You may not even realize it. But consider this: Talent is every nation's greatest resource. Without it, education falters, industries struggle, businesses close, and governments fall. I can pretty much guarantee there's an organization within 10 miles of your home struggling to find, keep, or train talent.

It's the Katie Mehnerts of the world who are working to keep your lights on and your home heated. Never, ever minimize the talent crisis in our midst. Talent generation influences your life. And if you're not helping to raise our next generation of talent, who is? Businesses, nonprofits, membership associations, governments, schools, and you have an opportunity—a responsibility—to become far more intentional and involved in talent generation.

## EY

One company that has excelled at raising talent is EY (formerly known as Ernst & Young). The original accounting firms founded by Alwin Ernst in 1906 and Arthur Young in 1903 merged in 1989 to form EY. With such a long history, and such a large employee base (231,000 employees), EY would be expected to fall into the category of legacy company, too steeped in tradition and too unwieldly in size to manage change.

Yet, EY's average employee age is 28, and the company describes itself as being bold, empowering innovation, and committed to building a better working world. What's the secret to their success? According to Natasha Stough, it's never leaning back or maintaining status quo. "That just isn't going to work. Not only for attracting students into professional services, but also for retaining them. You have to get comfortable with change and evolving your organization," she said.

Stough is Americas campus recruiting leader for EY, executing the firm's entry level hiring strategy of 11,000 students each year from campuses throughout North and South America. She joined the firm in 2005. "One of the reasons I've stayed at EY, quite frankly, is our leaders here at the firm push for change. And it can be uncomfortable. It can be challenging. But we need to continue to meet the needs of our clients and also provide and take great care of our people."

Stough referred to the importance of empathy. Boomers can be quick to shoot down flexibility or wearing headphones to work or jeans on Friday, but thinking more broadly about change, what it means to others, and being open to change is imperative to an organization's overall well-being, she noted.

EY also keeps the conversation going with the youngest generations—"because that's our next generation of talent"—such as hosting town halls with high school students. EY strives to identify talent early, getting to campus and talking to students early—even as young as their first or second year of college. The firm's renowned internship program has been in existence for more than 15 years, hiring students the year prior to graduation.

"We need to start branding the firm and the opportunities that we have early on, generate interest in some of our programs, as well as our internship program, because we very much need to build that pipeline of talent," Stough explained.

Being in continual dialogue and relationships with young people brings to light that their needs and interests differ from other generations, and as challenging as it can be, EY works to respond to these challenges. The firm recently expanded its parental leave benefits. Presently, EY is piloting a new performance management process. In the past, employees would set goals, then have a mid-year review and an annual review.

"Students coming out of college today want regular, intermittent feedback conversations," Stough said. So EY is piloting a program to provide regular feedback. One region is piloting Feedback Fridays, for which managers and partners share feedback on performance and areas of improvement with their teams each Friday. Thus far, the pilot's focus has been well-received for creating a means for less formal and more frequent dialogue.

EY has also been capable of change because the firm seeks out dynamic leaders. "Just because you're a great auditor, or because I'm a really great recruiter does not make either of us great leaders. Those are skills that you learn, develop, test, and try," Stough said.

She explained that EY focuses more on the development of high-performing teams to serve clients. People who lead at EY need to be strong and dynamic, so EY makes significant investments into the training and coaching of their high performers "to ensure we're developing the leaders of tomorrow."

EY continually shifts and changes to stay competitive and meet the needs of its global client base. "We have to push and we have to push in the right ways, whether it's creating innovative programs, developing our leaders, ensuring that we have high-performing teams. Those are things that we need to continue to focus on as we grow and evolve and change," Stough said.

EY is now embarking on a journey around strategic talent planning, contemplating how robotics, artificial intelligence, contingent workers, and data-analytics will both disrupt and complement EY's future workforce. This process is inclusive of conversations with universities and administrators in business, engineering, informatics, and technology. In brief, EY remains capable of change and relevance and talent generation because it's kept a people-first and future-focused process.

## The Future of Talent

While people may have expected Scott Wiley to launch programs geared toward recruiting college students and young professionals into the field of accounting, few imagined he would try to influence students still in high school.

"Our academic environment can't keep up with the business environment," Wiley said. He knew that if Ohio Society of CPAs (OSCPA) wanted to engage more talent in the field of accounting, he had to start young and he had to change the way children learned about accounting careers.

"We've got to change the public perception of what CPAs do. People think of CPAs and they imagine people wearing green-colored visors, hunkered over their desks. They think it's boring work and that's not the case at all. We want the public to know accountants have a broad range of skills and do interesting work," Wiley said.

So OSCPA invested into an accounting image campaign, started hosting career days at high schools, and began advocating for the introduction of an AP Accounting Course as an extension of the high school math curriculum. That's not an easy task considering most accounting classes are currently being taught by home economics or physical education teachers, Wiley noted. In addition, the OSCPA team started meeting with high school faculty, encouraging them to move students into accounting classes, and teamed up with some schools to bring young CPAs into high school classrooms. "Parents, counselors, teachers all need to know about accounting careers. STEM is making a full-court press, and we have to get accounting in there," Wiley said.

OSCPA is so sincere about transitioning the education experience, and aligning it with business needs, that the association is currently piloting a high school membership. Students aren't charged dues to be a student affiliate, but they do receive access to news and information about the profession, college scholarship opportunities, discounts on CPA exam review courses, access to the career center which lists internships and job opportunities, and invites to social events.

Each summer, OSCPA hosts a career-development program, giving high school students the opportunity to explore careers in accounting and business while spending a week on a college campus. It's like summer camp for accounting.

Wiley said some people have criticized his decision to offer a complimentary membership, but he explained his intentions aren't driven by revenue. "We don't just want students as members, we want to prepare them for a future in the profession. We're building relationships with them, preparing them, and giving them a competitive advantage," he said.

The high school initiative joins OSCPA's extensive suite of programs and benefits for college students and young professionals, ranging from a leadership academy to job shadowing, and a physical presence at 16 colleges and universities in the state of Ohio. In addition, OSCPA has started providing training programs for its member companies struggling to manage and develop young talent.

To Wiley, there's nothing more important than talent generation. Three full-time employees are devoted exclusively to resolving Ohio's accounting talent pipeline crisis. "We have to stay focused on what we want to achieve. If it doesn't fit within our vision, we don't do it. Focus means making decisions and realizing you can't be everything to everyone," he said.

"This work feels good and right. We should give back to the profession," Wiley said, adding that workforce development is the new normal for OSCPA and something the association will continue to dedicate resources towards resolving. "We're never going to be done with this."

## A Future to Create

A few years ago, I was a consultant on a project for Dollars for Scholars. Their founder's story is an absolute inspiration.

In 1957, Dr. Irving Fradkin was an optometrist practicing in Fall River, Massachusetts, a struggling former mill town. He had been struck by how few of his young patients planned to attend college, mostly because they could not afford it.

This bothered Fradkin and he set out to do something about it.

He figured that if each household in Fall River gave just one dollar (the equivalent of about $8 today), every graduating high school senior could be sent to college. The idea gave birth to Dollars for Scholars, a campaign he almost single-handedly began on a card table in his home, and by the end of 1958 (when tuition was typically well under $1,000 annually) it had delivered $5,000 to 24 local high school seniors.

Nearly 60 years later, it has evolved into Scholarship America, an organization that by its own estimate has overseen the distribution of $3.5 billion to more than 2.2 million students. Based in St. Peter, Minnesota, it also coordinates about 500 local Dollars for Scholars affiliates, which have awarded $600 million to about 750,000 students since 1958.

Dr. Fradkin was an unabashed fundraiser. He even called the White House to solicit support for Dollars for Scholars. He received congratulatory greetings from his home state senator, John F. Kennedy, and President Dwight D. Eisenhower, and received his first $1 from Eleanor Roosevelt.

In 2016, Dr. Fradkin died. He was 95. An editor in Providence, Rhode Island, authored an article recalling his memories of Dr. Fradkin, stating: "What I remember most about Fradkin was his indefatigable spirit and his optimism."

Indefatigable. That's what we need to be right now. If one man's determination can result in the education of 2.3 million students, imagine what your business, membership association, city, or school could do to solve the talent crisis. It must be a collective effort, and Wiley is right—we're never going to be done with this. The need for talent generation is here to stay.

The future of workforce development and leadership development will look like this:

- Students won't learn by memorization or be expected to master all subjects, rather schools will provide interactive learning opportunities and strengths-based education tracks;

- Schools will continually adapt their curriculum to introduce courses that reflect the needs of our workforce, such as STEM, robotics, coding, artificial intelligence, leadership, and entrepreneurism;

- Schools will also focus on specialized coursework and learning opportunities in our nation's high-demand fields, such as healthcare and manufacturing;

- High schools, colleges, and professional and trade associations will implement certification programs, ensuring highly specialized workforce-ready training in a short period of time;

- Industry and education will align in the development of curriculum and classes designed to train our workforce with the skills needed to compete successfully in the workplace;

- Businesses will actively participate in every level of the education process, from elementary school to college, providing field trips, job shadowing and internship opportunities, and providing instruction in the classroom;

- School boards will be composed of a mix of business leaders, educators, and students;

- Businesses will provide incubators to start-ups, as well as student projects and aspiring entrepreneurs;

- Professional and trade associations will provide education, job training, scholarships, and certifications to students;

- Businesses will provide grants to schools to provide specialized education and job training; and

- Membership associations will be a conduit for workforce development, bringing industry and education together.

This is just the beginning. The point is, we need to fast-track workforce development. Education needs to be revamped, businesses need to be more involved and put resources into training workers, and industries need to actively advocate to government and educational entities for the prioritization of relevant coursework, training, and workforce development programs.

A change is required, and reassessing how we raise talent is certainly part of the solution. Talent is our nation's greatest asset. A corporation is nothing without talent. A city, hospital, school, energy company, or accounting firm is nothing without talent. Talent is the heart and soul of every organization, and developing that talent has become more critical than ever.

Ladies and gentlemen, now is time to think about talent because our leadership is aging and our talent practices are failing. We cannot become a nation that relies on others to manufacture, create, and innovate. We cannot sit back and wait for our government or someone else to solve this problem. If we do, we continue to fail.

We cannot be comfortable with the status quo, resisting change and innovation and young talent. We cannot be apathetic towards our future, thinking it will be someone else's problem to solve. If we do, we continue to fail.

Talent generation isn't someone else's problem to solve. It's yours and it's mine. We're responsible for the future, and I don't want to mess it up—for me, for my children, for their children, and their children's children.

We can, and must, do better. We must work together to close the skills gap. We must equally invest in our workforce and take advantage of every opportunity to create a stronger, better trained, more engaged workforce.

We must be indefatigable.

**CHAPTER SUMMARY**

The switch over to the Talent Economy, mixed with the largest shift in human capital in history, has formed a perfect storm. Our workforce needs have forever shifted, and every entity everywhere is struggling to adapt, engage, and grow talent.

The perfect recipe for workforce development doesn't exist, because workforce development has never been a problem of this magnitude, breadth, or severity. But we can't afford to wait for someone else to do something. If we want to build a growing economy for generations to come, every organization has a role to play—be it a city, membership association, business, school, or government entity. We all must work to solve the skills gap and develop a strong foundation for today's workforce and generations to come.

**QUESTIONS TO CONSIDER**

1. Is your organization growing older or younger? Why?

2. Imagine your organization without talent, and being forced to close down. What's the worst thing that could happen?

3. How could you support workforce development in your industry/ workplace/city?

4. What steps will you take in the next six months to help retain or raise talent?

Reflect on the strategies you've learned in this book, and the traction that organizations gained when they put people first and became future focused. Consider who in your organization is most positive and passionate about the future success of your organization. Discuss the table topics below with them, identifying a vision and charting a course for your organization to get started on the path towards talent generation right away.

| Where we are | Where we want to be | Why this is important | What we will do and when |
|---|---|---|---|
|  |  |  |  |
|  |  |  |  |
|  |  |  |  |
|  |  |  |  |
|  |  |  |  |

# Index

**L**

Learning Sciences International, 220–221

Likeable Local, 177

LinkedIn, 48, 117, 135

Logan, Dave, 187

London Business School, 132

London Stock Exchange, 117

Loyd, Matthew, 111–113

Lyft, 134, 155–156

Lynda.com, 154

**M**

*Mad Men,* 172

*Made Magazine,* 208

Markitors, 85

Martin, Nicole, 35, 91

Massachusetts Biomedical Initiatives, 180

Massachusetts Institute of Technology, 220

Mayer, Melissa, 141–142

Mayham, Kenzie, 191

McKinsey & Company, 149, 186

Mehnert, Katie, 212–214, 226

Mentoring, 47–48
    reverse, 49–50
    micro, 51–52

MemberClicks, 190–192

Method, 111

MicroMentor, 51

Microsoft, 8, 53, 117, 136

Millennial Branding, 12

*Millennials in Adulthood,* 121

*Millennial Generation Research Review, The,* 121

Millennials to Members, 193

*Millennials: We Suck and We're Sorry,* 80

Minneapolis Regional Chamber of Commerce, 201

Minnesota Council on Foundations, 112, 163

Misfit, 111

*Misled: How a Generation of Leaders Lost the Faith,* 82

Morgan, Jacob, 131, 135–137

Moritz, Bob, 132, 165, 167

Mosaic, 53

Motivosity, 62–63

MSNBC, 99

**N**

Namely, 69

NASA, 140

NASDAQ, 123, 137

Nashville Area Chamber of Commerce, 204

National Environmental Health Association, 41–43

National Public Radio, 12

Netflix, 117

New Media Upstarts, 181

Newsweek, 23

New York Federal Reserve, 220

Nielsen, 183–184

Nike, 158

Nordstrom, 143–144

Novo Nordisk, 125

**O**

Obama, Barack, 171–172, 196

Ohio Society of CPAs, 199–200, 229–231

Old Navy, 111

Onreel.news, 177

OPEC, 212

Open Salaries Formula, 105

Optum, 50

Oxford University, 151, 219